MW01504743

E Marbell

3209 Angell Hall
U. of Michigan
Ann Arbor, MI 48109
_1003

SECURITY FOR AMERICA'S CHILDREN

PROCEEDINGS OF THE FOURTH CONFERENCE OF THE NATIONAL ACADEMY OF SOCIAL INSURANCE

PAUL N. VAN DE WATER
LISBETH B. SCHORR
Editors

KENDALL / HUNT PUBLISHING COMPANY
2460 Kerper Blvd. Dubuque, IA 52001

NATIONAL
ACADEMY
OF • SOCIAL
INSURANCE

ACKNOWLEDGMENTS

Many people were instrumental in turning the fourth annual conference of the National Academy of Social Insurance into this book. The planning committee, chaired by Lisbeth B. Schorr, included Robert M. Ball, Sarah S. Brown, Olivia Golden, Robert Greenstein, Pamela J. Larson, Sara Rosenbaum, Stanford G. Ross, C. Eugene Steuerle, and James Weill. Cassandra De Young and Alison Rapping prepared the manuscript for publication. Mendelle T. Berenson edited it. Marion Curry assisted with the typing. The conference was supported by grants from the Annie E. Casey Foundation and the Carnegie Corporation of New York.

P.N.V.

Other Conference Proceedings published by the National Academy of Social Insurance

Social Security and the Budget: Proceedings of the First Conference of the National Academy of Social Insurance (November 1989).

Retirement and Public Policy: Proceedings of the Second Conference of the National Academy of Social Insurance (January 1991).

Social Insurance Issues for the Nineties: Proceedings of the Third Conference of the National Academy of Social Insurance (January 1992).

Printed in the United States of America
10 9 8 7 6 5 4 3 2 1

THE NATIONAL ACADEMY OF
SOCIAL INSURANCE

T he National Academy of Social Insurance is a nonprofit, nonpartisan organization devoted to furthering knowledge and understanding of Social Security, protection against the cost of health care services provided for or required by government, unemployment insurance, disability insurance, workers' compensation, and related public and private programs.

The Academy provides a forum in which to explore challenges and opportunities facing the fields of social insurance and health care financing; assesses social insurance programs and their relationship to other public and private programs; helps develop scholars and administrative leaders; supports basic study, policy analysis, and research; and promotes public understanding of social insurance principles and programs. The Academy has 345 members, who represent a balance of disciplines and ideologies and who are recognized experts in social insurance and health care financing.

The Academy takes responsibility for assuring the independence of any project organized under its auspices. Participants in the fourth annual conference were chosen for their recognized expertise and with due consideration of the balance of disciplines appropriate to the program. The resulting proceedings represent the views of those who presented the papers and are not necessarily the views of the members of the National Academy of Social Insurance.

CONTENTS

Rethinking Children's Security: New Challenges for Social Insurance

Lisbeth B. Schorr and Paul N. Van de Water

T he idea of devoting the fourth annual conference of the National Academy of Social Insurance to children's income and health security came from the Academy's chair, Robert M. Ball. He saw the synergy in bringing the experts in income security for the retired, disabled, widowed, orphaned, and unemployed and the experts on health insurance together with those who focus on the needs of children. Indeed, the opportunity to think together and to exchange information across traditional boundaries proved enormously productive, and this volume of proceedings will allow a wider audience to share in and continue the discussion. Our introductory essay summarizes the papers presented at the conference and identifies the major themes that emerged from the deliberations.

Summary

In his opening remarks, David A. Hamburg suggests that nothing less than the future of the society is at stake in the questions addressed here: how to provide security for America's children, and how to design public policy to improve the circumstances in which children grow up.

Lisbeth B. Schorr is lecturer in social medicine at Harvard University and author of *Within Our Reach: Breaking the Cycle of Disadvantage.* Paul N. Van de Water is deputy assistant director for budget analysis at the Congressional Budget Office.

Paul Starr points out that the apparent agreement among politicians, business leaders, professionals, and commissions on the need to invest in children today is extraordinary. Not since the Progressive Era, he says, has social policy and public rhetoric concentrated such attention on the plight of America's children. He speculates that the apparent consensus around the proposition that significant new investments in children are morally right and economically sound may be in part illusory, actually obscuring deep and unresolved political differences. Concern for children may be a metaphor for our more general worries about the future, but it may also suggest the beginning of enough agreement to lead to a redirection of public policy.

Starr argues that our public and private social security systems no longer fit today's family structures and gender relations. He calls for "a New Deal for the young" that emphasizes universal rather than poverty-related programs. Elements of his program include a refundable tax credit for children, family leave, an increase in support for child care, financing of post-secondary education through the income tax system, child support assurance, national service, and universal health insurance.

James Weill and Theda Skocpol comment on the likelihood and feasibility of achieving Starr's New Deal for the young. Weill finds three positive forces already in place: an understanding of the need to make the workforce more productive, so that it can keep the nation competitive and support a large elderly population early in the next century; a growing recognition that childhood poverty has huge economic and social costs; and the end of the Cold War, which will allow our nation's energy to be redirected toward meeting its domestic needs. Skocpol contends that two more things are necessary: an emphasis on what she calls responsible parenting and a revitalized sense of civic responsibility and faith in public institutions.

Douglas J. Besharov, while not disagreeing with Starr's analysis, adds two major caveats. First, new public programs of child care or health benefits could prove to be extremely costly, yet not do much to improve the lot of children. The best way to do that, he says, is to improve the behavior of their parents. Second, the new-found concern for children could lead just as easily to more social control as to more social support.

Mary Jo Bane reviews the literature on the relation between family income and children's outcomes, such as educational attainment and early childbearing. She finds that the connection is weaker than might be expected. One reason is that other, more important variables, particularly parents' education, are highly correlated with income. But another reason, she concludes, is that not all sources of income are equally beneficial. In a two-parent family, the earnings of the family's head have a positive relation to outcomes. In a single-parent family, child support is the only income source that seems unambiguously to have positive effects. Bane therefore argues that guaranteed child support should be the cornerstone of welfare reform.

Gwendolyn S. King describes the Social Security Administration's role in helping needy children. Although not usually thought of as a children's program, Social Security—old-age, survivors, and disability insurance—provides almost as much money for children as does aid to families with dependent children (AFDC). Children who are from low-income families and who have a disability may be eligible for supplemental security income (SSI) benefits. Thanks to a major outreach effort and a revision of the disability criteria for children, children with disabilities represent the fastest-growing category of SSI recipients.

Children's Income Security

Three groups of papers examine ways to strengthen the three major sources of income for families with children: child support, earnings from work, and government transfer payments.

Child Support Payments. Newspapers and television have recently been full of stories about the inadequacies of current arrangements for child support. Many children fail to receive child support because their paternity has not been legally established. Even when the courts have established a child support obligation, many absent parents fail to make their payments. These problems affect not only the poor but the middle class as well.

Irwin Garfinkel calls for the establishment of a national child support assurance system. In this system, the child support obligation of the nonresident parent would be a percentage of his income, with the amount depending on the number of children. The obligation would be routinely withheld from his paycheck. The child's caretaker would receive either what the nonresident parent pays or an assured benefit, whichever is higher, and the government would make up any difference. Garfinkel contends that this system would foster the establishment of paternity, reduce poverty and dependence on welfare, and cost the taxpayer relatively little.

Earnings from Work. Current antipoverty efforts rely heavily on programs whose benefits are tied to a family's income. These means-tested programs minimize costs to the taxpayer by targeting public funds on the most disadvantaged. But they also discourage work because benefits are reduced as income grows. Efforts to reform welfare have frequently foundered in the attempt to reduce poverty, spur work, and contain costs all at the same time.

One way of reducing disincentives to work is to place greater reliance on universal programs, such as Garfinkel's child support assurance system, and less on means-tested programs. Even if the child support assurance system worked to perfection, however, half of the welfare caseload would remain. Other complementary policies would still be necessary.

A second approach to making work pay is to restructure AFDC by placing greater emphasis on helping welfare recipients to become self-sufficient. The Work Incentive program of 1967 (WIN), the WIN demonstration program of 1981, and the program of Job Opportunities and Basic Skills Training (JOBS) in the Family Support Act of 1988 embody this welfare-to-work strategy. WIN emphasized job search and rapid job placement. JOBS goes further and offers education, training, and child care services to help welfare recipients prepare for and hold a job. By 1995, states will have to provide these services to 20 percent of employable welfare recipients.

Judith Gueron finds substantial evidence that programs to encourage work among single mothers on AFDC can be successful. Extensive studies of WIN demonstrations during the 1980s, she reports, show sustained increases in employment and reductions in welfare receipt. Most of the people who went to work saw little increase in their incomes, however, because their earnings were largely offset by reductions in their welfare payments. The hope is that the JOBS program, by providing education, training, and other forms of support, will help people get markedly better jobs, yield larger increases in family incomes, and help achieve the promise of long-term self-sufficiency. But work-to-welfare programs will prove most effective, Gueron concludes, if further reforms outside the welfare system help make work pay.

Lawrence M. Mead contends that the main economic problem of poor families is their lack of work effort, not the failure of work to pay enough. Very few steady workers are poor. Conversely, fewer than one in five poor heads of households work full year and full time. And there is no evidence, Mead says, that higher wages or work-related benefits would induce poor people to work significantly more. Mead therefore argues for work requirements rather than work incentives. Like Gueron, Mead finds that recent work programs linked to welfare have succeeded in increasing employment and earnings, and he contends that expanding such programs is the most promising approach to improving the lot of the poor in the long run. As the next step in this direction, Mead concludes, it is vital to meet the 20 percent participation target for the JOBS program.

Isaac Shapiro differs with Mead on the importance of increasing the returns to work. Although they may represent only 2 percent of the population, he says, about 5.5 million people live in poor families with children that also have a full-time year-round worker. Moreover, as Mead's data show, many categories of the poor have increased their work effort since 1975. Shapiro recommends two major measures to improve the returns to work: expansion of the earned income tax credit (EITC) and an increase in the minimum wage. At present, even when combined with the EITC, full-time work at the minimum wage is not enough to lift a family out of poverty. The major argument against raising the minimum wage is that it would reduce job opportunities for low-skilled workers, but Shapiro cites several recent studies that suggest this argument is overstated.

Government Transfer Payments. Two panelists—Robert Greenstein and Rudolph G. Penner—addressed the question, What could $10 billion or $40 billion do for children?

Greenstein's $40 billion package comprises a child support assurance system (less than $10 billion), a refundable tax credit of $700 per child (about $20 billion), an expansion of housing certificates and vouchers ($5 billion to $8 billion), and less costly improvements in food stamps, AFDC, the dependent care tax credit, and other programs. If only $10 billion were available, Greenstein would drop the refundable children's credit and scale back the other elements of his plan.

Penner finds it impossible to imagine that $40 billion could become available to spend at a time when the federal budget deficit exceeds $300 billion. He therefore suggests a much more modest program that includes expansion of the earned income tax credit, an increase in the federal share of AFDC, relaxation of the asset test for AFDC, and a reduction of AFDC's implicit tax on child support payments.

In replying to the papers by Greenstein and Penner, Allan C. Carlson recommends spending $40 billion on a $1,000 refundable, indexed tax credit per child. He would use the refundable credit as a replacement for part of the federal contributions to AFDC and food stamps. Because both these programs are means tested, the plan would reduce disincentives to work and marriage; it would also minimize bureaucratic intrusiveness. A refundable child credit, Carlson argues, would also create a sense of solidarity between rich and poor families with children.

Disagreeing with Penner's contention that the United States cannot afford a major new investment in children, Olivia Golden says that the nation cannot afford *not* to reduce child poverty, and that the public must be persuaded to spend the necessary money. She generally agrees with Greenstein's proposals but would add up to six months of paid parental leave.

Margaret C. Simms questions Greenstein's and Penner's assumption that children need money more than anything else and that the market is an effective way of meeting children's needs. Even if parents had more money, the market might not supply the needed services, or the parents might not spend the additional money on the services that children need most.

Children's Health Security

Sarah S. Brown expresses a deep concern that reforming the financing of health care may not deal with the special needs of pregnant women and young children. Especially for these groups, access to health insurance is not the same as access to health care. She argues that any reform of the American health care system should emphasize primary and preventive care for children and pregnant women, offer them health care in appropriate settings (including school-based clinics and community health centers), increase the number and diversity of providers (including certified nurse-midwives and nurse-practitioners), preserve needed public health programs, design managed care arrangements to accommodate the special needs of mothers and children, and guarantee administrative simplicity.

Those who commented on Sarah Brown's paper generally agreed with its recommendations and tried to analyze why children's health has not been a top priority. Lawrence Brown cites the diffuse and fragmented nature of children's policy, which involves many different constituencies, bureaucracies, and programs. Charles N. Kahn, III, emphasizes Americans' lack of enthusiasm for redistributing income. And Bruce C. Vladeck blames animosity toward teenagers, especially black and Hispanic teenagers. Sara Rosenbaum suggests that these barriers may fall if coverage of dependents under employer-sponsored health insurance shrinks further and the cost of health care for children pinches more middle-class families.

Major Themes

What themes emerged from the papers, comments, and discussion at the conference? Despite the wide variety of backgrounds and perspectives of the participants, we discovered a much wider zone of agreement than might have been expected. There was clear agreement that the fix we are in today developed largely because the economic and social changes that endanger family security and children's well-being today have emerged so rapidly that the institutional arrangements that could prevent or mitigate the resultant casualties have not had time to evolve.

We were exposed to evidence that much is known about how to design some—not all, but some—of the institutions that would, indeed, respond to the changed circumstances of children and families today. John Palmer, the moderator of one session, pointed out that, in significant contrast with the past, we do have broad agreement with regard to both objectives and means. Much of the discussion suggested that the country is open to change as never before, both on income and on health security for children.

Assuring Child Support

The most resounding consensus coalesced around the need for, and the efficacy and appropriateness of, a major commitment to assure child support as part of the social insurance system, established in a pattern very much like survivors insurance. As Irwin Garfinkel observed, "If the architects of the Social Security Act could invent a social institution that assured that children were supported by their deceased parents, surely we can invent a social institution to assure that children are supported by their living parents."

The discussion made clear that we know how to assure child support. Moreover, that program responds to the calls for greater parental responsibility for children, it increases family income without a work disincentive and without massive federal outlays, and it can reduce the number of those who are dependent on AFDC. On top of all that, Mary Jo Bane assures us, child support is the source of income that is most unambiguously associated with improvements in life outcomes!

Budget Constraints

Most of the speakers who explored ways of allocating new resources to curb damage to the young seemed to agree that in addition to funding assured child support, the new money should go to a refundable tax credit for children; to expansion and simplification of the earned income tax credit; and probably to a more generous AFDC—a program that might nevertheless be smaller overall because child support assurance, the tax credit, and the JOBS program would permit many recipients to leave its rolls.

We heard about the strong and consistent findings that welfare-to-work programs have been successful, even when operated in large public bureaucracies and even in the face of economic disincentives to leave welfare for work. Judith Gueron laid out evidence indicating that if work became more attractive economically, even more people would leave welfare.

Making Work Pay

The ways that public policy could make work pay also seemed to be widely agreed on, although Lawrence Mead disputed the need for additional work incentives. Making work pay may mean an increase in the minimum wage; it also means an expanded earned income tax credit, child support assurance, increased support for child care, paid parental leave, and health benefits that are not tied to welfare status or low income. An alternative, favored by Allan Carlson, is to replace means-tested benefits as much as possible with a refundable tax credit for children. These measures were seen as constructive responses to the anger the middle class expresses because they perceive—whether or not justly—that the poor are not exercising individual responsibility or bearing their fair share of social obligations. Moreover, they answer those concerns with fewer damaging consequences than would cuts in welfare payments.

Universal and Targeted Programs

Many spoke about the barriers to meeting the needs of children and their families that will remain as long as the body politic considers the beneficiaries of public programs as other from themselves. Voters may see children as other because they have none of their own, or because many of the children in greatest need are poor or minority, or because they still think of each family as a boat that can more or less float on its own.

Today, *all* families need help from outside. Poor families need more help, especially if their children are to climb out of disadvantage and into self-sufficiency. The policy problem is tricky: We need a sense of community to extend universal programs into the seamless web of social policies that Theda Skocpol talks about. At the same time, Allan Carlson emphasizes, we need universal programs to send the message that we all have a common stake.

The policy problem is also tricky because, as Robert Greenstein points out, we need a mix of universal and targeted programs if we are to assist those who are hardest to reach at affordable costs. We can *reduce* the numbers dependent on non-universal programs, but not to zero. The very fact that a growing proportion of poor children are living in deep isolation and in dense concentrations of the persistently poor calls for special ways to reach them with the supports essential to their well-being.

Health Security

Paul Starr, Sarah Brown, and the panelists discussing health care reform all raised, explicitly or implicitly, the question of whether insurance is the appropriate framework for financing health care for children and pregnant women. That question arises because the primary objective here is not to insure against the risks of unexpected costs, but rather to ensure the effective delivery of routine preventive care. Neither the insurance model nor the current health care system fits the health care needs of mothers and children.

Many participants recognized Sarah Brown's nightmare that the decisions about health care reform will be settled without reference to the special needs of mothers and children, or to the special opportunities to meet those needs in more effective and less costly ways. But Henry Aaron suggested another nightmare: What if our efforts on behalf of children's health care create political obstacles to reform of health care financing and to cost containment?

However, with adroit designs for attaining them, these goals can be made highly compatible with one another. Better programs for pregnant women and children, far from compromising reform of health care financing and cost containment, may promote them. For example, capitation of comprehensive primary care for children and pregnant women can be seen as a way to adjust the poor fit between children's needs and the health insurance model. Such a carving out of primary care would reflect a growing sense that children are the responsibility of the whole society, not simply of their families and of employers. Moreover, it would acknowledge that health services for these groups go beyond the biomedical, and that combining them with social services and education enhances their effectiveness.

Making Common Cause with Other Sectors

Bruce Vladeck talks about the crisis in education, child welfare, and other human services as highly relevant to discussions of child health. The appetite for fundamental reform in all of these sectors is growing. Vladeck suggests discarding the medical care rubric for some basic health services and making common cause with these other sectors. There are serious tradeoffs here, of course; one risks losing access to significant sums of money. On the other hand, communities all over the country are considering proposals to deliver preventive health services, family planning, and prenatal care in non-health settings—in preschool programs, schools, family support programs, and the like. Head Start, of course, already incorporates certain health and nutrition services; schools may soon become sites of comprehensive services for pregnant women and for children beginning at birth, including child care, home visits by nurses, support of parents, and child welfare.

The High Stakes in Health Cost Containment

Meeting the health care needs of mothers and children and reforming health insurance may well require different contexts. Even so, that reform has great relevance for social policy for children and families. Paul Starr points out that the increases in health costs of the last three decades have crowded out other social programs. In 1965, the United States was spending 6 percent of its gross national product on each of three sectors: defense, education, and health. Today, defense is below 6 percent and falling. Education is still at 6 percent. And health care absorbs 14 percent of GNP. Those numbers make clear our common stake in intensifying rather than damping the pressure that is now behind health insurance reform and cost containment.

Conclusion

The papers and comments in this volume make visible the high degree of informed consensus around the need to adapt our social institutions to today's realities if we are to check the rate of casualties among children that threaten our future as a productive society. They also demonstrate that many of the policy tools needed to accomplish our objectives are already available.

We hope that this conference has contributed to a sense of social solidarity that includes a shared responsibility to all our children and to the families that struggle to raise them. If it has done so, it will have supplied not only the information for making decisions, but also the impetus to act on what we now know.

PART I

THE HISTORY AND CONTEXT

CHILDREN'S SECURITY
AND THE NATION'S FUTURE

David A. Hamburg

After World War II the immense preoccupation with the well-being of children caused Philip Wiley to speak of the United States as a pediarchy. Today, however, the attention we give to the various generations is out of kilter. We have shifted massive resources and much of our attention away from children and toward adults. As a result, the future of the country is at risk.

Let me begin by stating my basic outlook: What people do early in life lays the base for their entire lifespan. The early years can build a foundation for a long, healthy life, characterized throughout its course by curiosity and learning. Health and education are closely linked in the development of vigorous, skillful, and adaptable young people. Guided by research in the biomedical and behavioral sciences, investments in health and education can prevent much of the damage now being done to children and adolescents and contribute substantially to a dynamic economy and a flourishing democratic society in the next century.

That outlook requires everyone in a caretaking role to ask certain basic questions: Does a child have a family? If not, what can be done to build a family or something like a family? What sort of help does this child need? How can it be arranged? Who is available to perform what we might call family-equivalent functions? Who can be mobilized to offer sustained individual attention—attachment, protection, encouragement, stimulation, and guidance?

David A. Hamburg is president of the Carnegie Corporation of New York.

If we provide answers to those questions, we will make a fundamental contribution to health and education for a lifetime. Health and education are bound tightly together in the successful development of children and adolescents, and the social environment powerfully influences both. These interrelationships complicate the social insurance approach to children, but it simply will not do to limit intervention to a traditional medical mode. Such interventions are only a part—albeit an important part—of healthy development.

Changes in the Structure of Families

The conditions of child rearing have changed drastically in recent years. Americans are far more likely now than they were three decades ago to postpone marriage, to bypass marriage, to live alone, to divorce, to have both parents working outside the home when the children are young, and to raise children alone as single parents. The past three decades have also seen a remarkable change in the patterns of contact between children and their adult relatives. Mothers are home much less, and there is little evidence of a compensating increase in the time fathers spend at home. Only about 5 percent of American children see a grandparent regularly—a much lower proportion than was the case in earlier times.

Thus, the mother is out of the home working, and the father and the grandparents are not compensating. Networks of social support that are essential to promoting education and health throughout childhood and adolescence are no longer accessible. At the same time, the rapidity of technological and social change has made the transition from infancy to adulthood increasingly difficult.

The obvious response to this problem is to have others, outside the family, perform the functions that parents or relatives formerly performed. But we are at an early stage in this great shift from home- to society-based functions, and the demand for high-quality child care far exceeds the supply. Even affluent families must be resourceful, skillful, and persistent to find quality care outside the home for their children. For young, single, poor, or minority parents, finding good child care is a nearly insuperable task.

Preventive Intervention

The Carnegie Corporation has come to focus on two formative but particularly vulnerable periods of life—infancy and early adolescence. These are times of rapid biological development. Many factors must come together harmoniously in these two periods if a child is to develop into a mature, productive adult, and right now that conjunction often fails.

What educational and health policies can limit the casualties of early childhood and adolescence that we now see multiplying? We need to consider education and health as a continuum extending from conception into adulthood. This continuum should include these elements:

- Enriched prenatal care
- Pediatric health care with a strong emphasis on prevention
- High quality daytime child care
- Preschool education, such as Head Start
- Parental education and support.

A recent report by the National Institutes of Health and the Public Health Service describes the expanded vision of prenatal care that some of us have long been advocating. Medical care remains the core of this approach, but it also includes a strong element of education and, for poor women particularly, social support. The emphasis is, first, on reaching out to women and educating them so that they will receive care beginning early in pregnancy. The next step is to teach prospective parents to care for themselves and their newborn baby—and to consider options for the course of life. This approach requires the ready availability of a dependable person who can provide social support for health and education throughout the months of pregnancy and beyond.

Preschool education should also place heavy emphasis on parental involvement and health services, as in the Head Start program. Good preschool education is not just a matter of stimulating young children's cognitive development. Children must also be ready for school socially and physically.

Our society may not need new institutions to facilitate child and adolescent development. The need, rather, is to find creative ways to use the existing community systems—schools, community organizations, and churches—to promote lifelong health and learning.

Costs of Intervention

What will it cost to save our children, rich and poor alike? A rational sequence of interventions of the kind I have been sketching, based on scientific research, professional experience, and humane values, cannot be implemented without substantial investment.

The first and most crucial investment, however, is not financial. It is what we might call parental investment in children—or its equivalent. Children need attachment, protection, guidance, stimulation, and help in coping with adversity. If, for all the reasons we have noted, they cannot have them from their parents, we must devise social arrangements that will reliably give them these vital supports.

Also, we can make wiser use of the currently available funds. Much of the money devoted to education and child health is not well spent. Replacing inadequate services—for example, poor school systems with inflated administrative structures—with better ones would ultimately cost less, not more, and would ensure better outcomes. Such changes must, of course, be undertaken case by case and place by place. But it is likely that adopting a more rational, integrated sequence of interventions could greatly reduce the costs of child development programs.

Our current approach to child and adolescent development already entails many social and economic costs: low productivity, poor skills, high costs of health care, bulging prisons, and a badly ripped social fabric. One way or another, society pays.

Wise investment in human capital is the most fundamental and productive investment any society can make. It is more important than oil or minerals, office buildings or factories, roads or weapons. All of these and much more depend on the quality of human resources and the decency of human relations. If these deteriorate, all else declines.

I see hopeful signs that, as a nation, we are awakening to the gravity of the problems of today's children. We can strengthen our research on child development, health, and education. And, armed with knowledge and experience, we can, without a doubt, construct more effective interventions for all our children. We have accomplished more difficult tasks in this country. We must now have the decency and the vision to invest in our children. Thereby we invest in our future.

A NEW DEAL FOR THE YOUNG

Paul Starr

N> ot since the Progressive Era has the plight of America's children received such concentrated attention. Countless reports, books, documentaries, and speeches have described and deplored the condition of America's children and urged a new national commitment to improving children's lives. Everyone says we need to invest in children, and that such investments not only are morally right but make economic sense—and they do.

Indeed, we have so great a consensus on behalf of children's interests—so broad, so emphatic, so well reasoned, so amply documented—that it is astonishing that we have so little to show for it. Of course, we all know children don't vote (unfortunately, a lot of their parents don't either). But perhaps we have little to show because much of the consensus is illusory, and we have yet to synthesize the diverse ideas for reform into a single compelling message and program. I want to suggest one way to do that.

Why Children?

Whenever a consensus about public policy emerges, it is subject to several interpretations. At least three interpretations of this consensus about the plight of children seem plausible. One is that people are creatively misunderstanding each other—that the consensus is superficial and obscures deeper political differences.

Paul Starr is a professor of sociology at Princeton University.

A second possibility is that different groups are using the problems affecting children to symbolize moral and political worries only tenuously related to children—that just as parents project their fears and hopes on their children, so do we as a nation.

Yet a third possibility is that we are in the midst of a veritable children's movement, on the verge of a genuine redirection of public policy and a reversal of the adverse trends affecting children's lives.

These three possibilities are not mutually exclusive. In the consensus about children, we may have all three—a misunderstanding, a metaphor, and a movement.

The misunderstanding—the deceptive consensus—is evident in the discussion of America's schools. It is striking how eagerly both the right and the left have embraced evidence about school failure. For different reasons, both conservatives and liberals have found it useful to hold the public schools responsible for problems of motivation, discipline, and performance that do not begin in school and that schools may not be able to remedy. Conservatives want to make public schools *private*; liberals want to make public schools *equal*. Neither side yet has the political capacity to get its way, and it seems unlikely that they can agree on making schools both more private *and* more equal. The school criticism and reform of the last decade, therefore, may turn out to represent no more than a consensus of convenience that fails to bring any breakthrough in policy.

Children are also clearly a metaphor for the nation's uneasiness about its future. We would not be hearing as much about children today if it were not for worries about national decline. As the Soviet Union's launch of Sputnik prompted a spurt of interest in education in the 1950s, so today we are reexamining educational and children's policies out of anxiety about our capacity to stand up to international competition. Much of the concern about children also reflects cultural anxiety about the decline of the family.

And yet, out of cross-purposes and a mixture of economic and cultural anxieties, some real support—an authentic movement—has developed for new policies affecting families and children. While highlighting the political and subjective elements in the new consensus, I do not mean to suggest that it lacks an objective foundation. We are all now familiar with the spread of poverty among children. We know about the shifts in family structure, the growing rates of illegitimacy, divorce, and single parenthood. We know, too, about the changes in the distribution of income, particularly the decline in the earnings of young workers, which affects their ability to raise children and probably their willingness to form families. Finally, we know about the trends in public expenditures that over the past several decades have reduced poverty and improved access to health care for the aged yet have left children and young families in distress.

Single parenthood and child poverty have also spread in Europe, although to a lesser extent. The problems of income security and health care tend to be more accentuated in the United States because of the historic weakness of family policy, the lack of universal health insurance, and the distinctive character of American conservativism, with its stricter devotion to free market ideology. So although many countries have entered a new post-industrial era in social policy, as Senator Daniel P. Moynihan suggests, the United States has developed a distinctive post-industrial social pattern, shaped by the institutions it has inherited from the past. [1]

Institutions That No Longer Fit

America's institutions were not conceived with today's world in mind. In particular, yesterday's public and private social security systems no longer fit today's family structures and gender relations.

Michael Young, now Lord Young, who worked on the original Beveridge plan half a century ago, said in a recent talk in London that the designers of the postwar welfare state did not concern themselves with the possibility that the problems of children and families might change; they presumed that traditional family structures would remain intact. The same may be said of our New Deal—for example, the provisions for women under the old-age insurance program and the expectations and presumptions behind aid to families with dependent children (AFDC). It is true as well of the design of the workplace and employer-sponsored benefit plans.

The old-age insurance program envisioned a single-earner family in which the woman's pension entitlement would depend upon her husband's contributions. The system does not deal appropriately or fairly today with married working women, whose Social Security contributions often do not affect their benefit entitlement.[2] AFDC assumed that women would become single parents primarily through widowhood; it did not envision the enormous expansion in the number of single-parent families arising from higher rates of divorce and illegitimacy. The design of the workplace assumed that mothers would be home taking care of children and that no special arrangements for youngsters were required. As ever more women work outside the home, we have to rethink the design of all these institutions.

---

1. Moynihan (1989).
2. Boskin (1986).

Consider employer-sponsored health insurance, which makes children and women outside the labor force only incidental, indirect, and insecure beneficiaries. This system has deteriorated sharply in recent years. According to a recent report of the Children's Defense Fund based on data from the Current Population Survey, the proportion of children with employer-based coverage dropped from 73 percent to 63 percent between 1977 and 1987. As of the summer of 1990, more than 25 million children—about 40 percent of all children—lacked employer-based coverage. The report predicts that 43 percent of the 46 million children who had coverage that summer will go without any insurance for some period by November 1992.[3]

The shrinkage of employment-based health benefits has been partly offset by the expansion of Medicaid eligibility for poor children, one of the few significant expansions in health coverage of the past decade. But for low-income working families who are ineligible for Medicaid, the decline of employment-based coverage is an ominous development.

The system for financing health care for most American children simply does not guarantee them security of coverage. Employers are not required to offer insurance for dependents, employees are not required to buy it when it is offered, and neither employers nor employees can control the spiral of costs that is undermining the insurance system and eroding the benefits. With rising health costs, the interests of children have been especially easy to sacrifice—even though children are the least expensive to care for.

I do not even think that insurance is the appropriate conceptual framework for financing health care for children. The objective should be not simply to insure against the risks of unexpected costs (which is the premise of the insurance model), but also to provide for routine, preventive care. Our health insurance system and the forms of medical service that have grown up in response to its incentives do not perform those preventive functions well at all, or they perform them at unreasonable cost. That is why, in thinking about national health insurance, it will not be enough simply to expand insurance coverage for children; we need to revamp the financing and provision of children's health services.

One alternative, under a universal insurance system, would be to create a mechanism for capitation payment of comprehensive child health services, which would be separate from the menu of options offered to adults. In other words, when signing up for a health plan, families would make two choices—one for adults, one for children—not a single choice for the entire family, as they do today. By separating the

---

3. Rosenbaum (1992).

choice for children, this approach would encourage health plans to compete for children and thereby promote attention to children's services. Moreover, it would permit the development of capitation plans—perhaps with clinics based in schools—focused on children's health. And by separating children's enrollment from that of the adults, it would allow parents who prefer a conventional indemnity arrangement for themselves to enroll their children in a health maintenance organization or school-based children's health service that had a greater capacity to address preventive, educational, and behavioral needs. Such an approach would be far more beneficial to children—and, ultimately, to the adults they become—than merely providing more money for high-tech medical intervention. Unfortunately, many think only of extending the employment-based health insurance system, not revising it; and the special concerns of children's health rarely come up at all.

Symbolic Politics or Social Reform?

As difficult as it seems, children's health care is probably an easier problem than children's poverty. The underlying economic trends eroding the earnings of young families with children seem to be extremely powerful, and the uncomprehending response of a large part of the public is to attribute the cause to the poor themselves—not to children, of course, but to their parents. Conservatives claim that poverty today is more behavioral than structural—that it results chiefly from the indulgence and permissiveness of the welfare system and from a moral decay that causes family decline, drug use, and violence. As Vice President Quayle put it in the wake of the Los Angeles riots, the poor suffer from a "poverty of values."

This is symbolic politics, in which the object is not to provide any solution but to exploit the poor to evoke and direct widely felt anxieties. No doubt the right-wing agenda of family values, with its attacks on homosexuality, pornography, and promiscuity and its defense of the traditional family, resonates powerfully among many Americans. But, at its best, it is an expression of indignation and anger, with little rational relation of means and ends. (At its worst, it is an expression of cynicism with a very clear relation of political means to a political end: encouraging the middle class majority to identify the poor as morally separate.) Even if the restoration of traditional family forms were our leading objective, would the means advocated by the right accomplish that goal? In reality, no one has any idea how to reverse the trends toward family breakup and illegitimacy. Ironically, if anyone has illusions about the power of public policy, it is those conservatives who think that the traditional family will recover its strength as a result of bans on pornography, discrimination against gays, and rules pushing welfare recipients to marry. In the history of social engineering, this is surely one of the more hopeless crusades.

But if the hopes are illusory, the consequences of cultural conservatism are real enough, as evidenced in the recent surge of punitive welfare policies. To some extent, these policies are recession related, inspired simply by budget cutting. But they also respond to and exploit a very real anger in the middle class about programs that seem not to require of the poor the obligations and responsibilities that others have to bear.

We must address those holding these views and recognize that their demand for responsibility has a reasonable basis. We have no choice but to fit social reform to public values, to accept what the sociologist Alvin Gouldner called "the norm of reciprocity."[4] If political citizenship imposes obligations as well as creating rights, so, too, does social citizenship. It is not a mistake, therefore, to make some benefits contingent on the performance of obligations, including work and participation in training programs, although we need to be careful to prevent the sins of parents from being visited on their children. This is the premise of Governor Clinton's "New Covenant," with its emphasis on providing more opportunity in line with greater responsibility.

Fitting social reform to public values means, as David Ellwood has emphasized, shifting the emphasis of income security programs to making work pay, rather than calling, as so many did in the 1960s, for welfare rights or a negative income tax.[5] The earned income tax credit exemplifies that idea, as do several other reforms I mention below. Making work pay involves creating a symbolic politics in the service of social reform instead of a symbolic politics that is a substitute for social reform. Those symbols should support what I call "a New Deal for the young."

A New Deal for the Young

The phrase "a New Deal for the young" calls attention to both the continuities and discontinuities with the original New Deal. The continuity is that the next New Deal should emphasize universal, nonracial social remedies, as against the more race-conscious policies and poverty-related programs that became important beginning in the 1960s. The difference, of course, is that the next New Deal should be conceived in the

---

4. Gouldner (1973).
5. Ellwood (1988).

light of the new structure of families and the changed relations of men and women, and that it should do for young families and children what the social insurance programs of the New Deal have done so successfully for the aged.

Increasing income support for young families through the tax system is clearly a primary part of such a strategy. A tax credit for children, in place of the current exemption, as proposed by Senator Albert Gore and Congressman Thomas Downey, is the right approach. Since the late 1940s, the value of the tax exemption for children has been sharply eroded; by steeply increasing the exemption or, even better, by providing a tax credit, we would be restoring the interests of the family in the tax code. Making the child care tax credit refundable would also help, and stepping up the earned income tax credit for children should prove politically acceptable, even though increasing welfare benefits for extra children is under attack.

Family leave, an increase in support for child care, and financing of postsecondary education through the income tax system—as proposed by Senator Bill Bradley and by Barry Bluestone and his colleagues—are other reforms that belong in the next New Deal.[6]

Child support assurance, as a partial replacement for welfare, also illustrates the potential for establishing a new foundation for social benefits that corresponds better both to current family patterns and to the moral demand for greater paternal responsibility.[7]

Likewise, national service responds to the demands for responsibility and obligation and would help strengthen the sense of a common social citizenship.

Finally, we need universal health insurance, which is important not only to improve health care but also to release resources for other social programs. In recent decades, the growth of spending on health has crowded out other social expenditures. In 1965, the United States spent around 6 percent of gross national product on each of three sectors: defense, education, and health. As of 1992, defense is 5 percent of GNP and falling, education is still about 6 percent, and health care is projected to absorb 14 percent of GNP. Since 1981, we have transferred 5 percent of GNP to health care—almost the equivalent of the entire defense budget. In this same period, the share of national income spent on health care in Western Europe and Canada, under national health insurance, has been flat or has increased only slightly. (The average for industrialized countries is 7.5 percent of GNP.) Unless we adopt a national health insurance program with tight budget constraints that fundamentally alters the

---

6. Bluestone and others (1990).
7. Garfinkel (1992).

incentives in the health care system, all other social programs are threatened. The basic ingredients of what some have called a neo-New Dealism. It is an approach conscious of our historical achievements in social insurance, but also of their limitations and the need to push beyond them. Several years ago some attempted to undermine the principles of Social Security under the banner of generational equity. We need to fulfill the aspirations of Social Security under the banner—and in the interests—of generational equity. Instead of creating intergenerational conflict, we must build a new intergenerational alliance to achieve a New Deal for the young.

References

Bluestone, Barry, and others. "Generational Alliance: Social Security as a Bank for Education and Training," *American Prospect,* no. 2 (Summer 1990), pp. 15–29.

Boskin, Michael J. *Too Many Promises: The Uncertain Future of Social Security.* Homewood, Ill.: Dow-Jones Irwin, 1986.

Ellwood, David. *Poor Support: Poverty in the American Family.* New York: Basic Books, 1988.

Garfinkel, Irwin. "Bringing Fathers Back In," *American Prospect,* no. 9 (Spring 1992), pp. 74–83.

Gouldner, Alvin W. "The Norm of Reciprocity," *American Sociological Review,* vol. 20 (April 1960). Reprinted in Alvin W. Gouldner. *For Sociology.* New York: Basic Books, 1973.

Moynihan, Daniel Patrick. "Toward a Post-Industrial Society," *Public Interest,* no. 96 (Summer 1989), pp. 16–27.

Rosenbaum, Sara, and others. "Children and Health Insurance." Washington: Children's Defense Fund, January 1992.

COMMENTS

James Weill

P aul Starr suggests that children are a metaphor for the nation's decline. I want to argue that, more important, children are the leading edge of the real decline in this nation. In this still enormously wealthy nation, one in four young children today lives in poverty. The incidence of low-birth-weight births, teen pregnancy, homeless or doubled-up living, child abuse and neglect, violence by and against children, school failure, and drug abuse is staggering. In the available international comparisons, the United States typically lags almost all other wealthy industrial democracies, and sometimes lags dozens of developing countries as well. A nonwhite one-year old in this country is less likely to be immunized than a child in 69 other countries.

How have we reached this parlous state?

Stagnation Since the Early 1970s

A key turning point came in the early 1970s. The United States entered then a period of profound economic, cultural, political, and demographic upheaval that has continued to this day. The nation also entered this period with just about the weakest set of supports for families and children of any affluent western nation. We had no national health insurance, no child allowances, no broad housing allowances, no system of parental leave (paid or unpaid), and no child care system—none of the social supports that families in other western nations had

James Weill is general counsel of the Children's Defense Fund.

come to expect. American families and children were thereby left particularly vulnerable to the economic changes of the last two decades.

At the same time, slower economic growth, a backlash against the civil rights movement, and a shift in political power away from families with children and the poor made it virtually impossible to achieve the major advances in social welfare policy we needed in those areas where we lagged the most. Demographic, political, and economic change prevented the institution of major new programs—supports that would have helped us catch up with our foreign peers and competitors— at precisely the time that the need for new supports became greatest.

For example, young families suffered huge income losses and increases in their poverty rates during the 1970s and 1980s. But even though those young families were helped the least by the preexisting social welfare system, they grew more and more powerless politically to erect new public buffers against the disasters they faced in the market economy. Their incomes fell at the same time as money came to play a more prominent role in politics and the formulation of public policy. They became a smaller and smaller share of the population. And they further diffused their political power by becoming alienated, rather than coalescing as a political force.

Continued Stalemate in the 1980s

All these trends made the social welfare programs, as inadequate as they already were, vulnerable to spasms of deep retrenchment, such as the budget cuts of 1981. Those cuts were deepest not only in means-tested programs for families but also in social insurance benefits for children, as was seen in the elimination of Social Security student benefits.

But the 1981 cuts, as disastrous as they were, pale in comparison to the stalemate in social policy that has continued for two decades. Our society has been unable to build substantial new programs. We have fought over scraps from the table. The policy stalemate has made it impossible to compensate for declining real wages, rising rates of out-of-wedlock births, rising divorce rates, and the increasingly contingent nature of many new jobs; and it has often exacerbated the effects of these trends. Young adults often can find only service jobs that are part-time or temporary, or even if they are full-time, are untenured and lack benefits. It is hardly surprising, then, that the last two decades have produced a large shift of income, not just from the young to the middle-aged and the elderly but from families with children to families without children.

Are we going to be able to break out of this stalemate? As Paul Starr suggested, some of the consensus on meeting children's needs is deceptive. It is not mere coincidence, for example, that, in the January 1992 State of the Union Address, one of the few programs President Bush was willing to propose cutting was a program for poor children—aid to families with dependent children. But many of the current proposals to cut AFDC, allegedly to encourage smaller families, discourage moving for benefits, and promote work effort, are wholly symbolic and politically motivated. Studies show that families on welfare are the same size as other American families and that welfare benefits have no effect on migration. AFDC already has enforceable requirements for work and training, but the nation lacks enough good jobs at good wages to make those requirements meaningful.

The debate must not be about welfare but about race, wages, poverty, and the future of our children. Although we need reciprocity in our welfare programs between recipients' rights and recipients' responsibilities, we need real reciprocity, not posturing. We should not hurt children while we fight out the politics of race and poverty in the adult population.

Support for change has been growing in the business, academic, and philanthropic communities, but reform is still trailing far behind the rhetoric. The strong, bipartisan report of the National Commission on Children, *Beyond Rhetoric*, is obviously an important step forward. But we are making little if any progress toward enacting family leave and national health insurance into law. Even the effort to improve schools and readiness for school—the area of most sweeping consensus—has not yet achieved traction. Poor and minority schools are being left further behind, and Head Start is less than one-third of the way to full funding.

Forces for Change in the 1990s

In light of all this inertia, how will we achieve Paul Starr's New Deal for the young?

Some compelling forces are moving us ahead. First come the demographic trends. A shrinking cohort of young workers will have to support a growing elderly population, and those workers will have to be skilled, productive, and working in well-paid jobs to do so and to keep this nation competitive. Although that argument has so far achieved mostly symbolic meaning, it is an argument that must come to have real meaning for the American people and the future of this economy.

Second, there is growing recognition that the high poverty rates for children, not only in the inner cities but in rural and suburban areas, have huge economic and social costs. They drive up our school dropout and our teen pregnancy rates. They drive up our infant mortality rates and our health costs. To move the debate forward, these and other costs of child poverty must be quantified and publicized.

The greatest source of hope, however, should be the end of the Cold War—one of those turning points in history that calls out for great endeavors. I am hopeful not simply because the Cold War's end should free up billions of dollars previously spent on defense. Those billions will help, but they are not going to be enough to meet all of this country's deferred domestic needs. Rather, what is important about the end of the Cold War should be the energy that it frees up.

The real peace dividend will be an explosion of attention to our unmet domestic needs. For almost one-fifth of its life, this nation has expended much of its energy, and located much of its identity, ideology, and sense of national cohesion in the Cold War. The end of the Cold War offers the opportunity to recapture and redirect much of that energy, identity, and national purpose toward addressing this country's wide range of domestic needs.

At the head of the line must come the nation's children and families. We must create social insurance and social welfare systems that support work, provide generous assistance to families, and give families a base on which to build better lives. I have argued that children's status is not just a metaphor for the nation's decline but that it is also the leading edge of the nation's decline. Meeting children's needs must therefore become the leading edge not only of the nation's economic resurgence but also of a resurgence of confidence and pride in the course our nation is taking.

COMMENTS

Theda Skocpol

B ecause I agree with Paul Starr's analysis, I want to focus on the issue that James Weill raised: the political feasibility of a New Deal for children or, as some of us have called it, a family security program.

Children have universal appeal. Wanting to help the innocent seems automatic. Moreover, Americans have always valued youth; it symbolizes openness and opportunity for building in the future. It is indeed interesting that this metaphor comes to the fore in a period when we are worried about our future, as Paul Starr pointed out.

American children today, especially those in poverty or in single-parent families, also have great needs. It is easy to document those needs, and it is easy to make a rationally compelling argument about the cost effectiveness of helping children.

Nevertheless, looking back over the history of American social policy from the nineteenth century to the present, we can see that there are also some important obstacles to creating public policies to help children, despite the evident moral and logical appeal of doing so.

Why Haven't Children Fared Better?

First, the elderly—not advocates of children—have been well organized politically and have made themselves the chief beneficiaries of public largesse. That has been true from the time of benefits for Civil War veterans in the late nineteenth and early twentieth centuries

---

Theda Skocpol is a professor of sociology at Harvard University.

through the Social Security old-age insurance program, which was the most splendid social policy achievement of the New Deal. The elderly were also the chief beneficiaries of the War on Poverty and the Great Society. Despite the ostensible focus of many of the Great Society programs on improving life for children, youth, and young adults, the primary beneficiaries of the programs proved to be the elderly.

Second, other nations have often found it easier than the United States has to emphasize helping children because, for demographic reasons often tied to military competition, they have wanted more children. In the United States the desire for more children has never been a strong factor fueling public policy. Differences of ethnicity and race, as well as issues of immigration, have repeatedly stirred worries that the wrong people would be encouraged to have more children if public policies were designed to help families with children. Those worries, unpleasant as they are to think about, remain very much with us today in popular discourse and in segments of elite discourse.

Third, children are always seen as parts of families. This is nowhere more true than in America, where rights of privacy are emphasized. Helping children also means helping the adults who bear them and care for them. Are the adults who will be helped by child-centered policies effective political actors? Are they appealing objects of aid, or can they be made to seem appealing? Often Americans seem to answer no, as when more generous welfare policies are proposed.

The last great child-centered era in American social policy was the Progressive Era, and there is a very important difference between then and now. Then, mothers and children were understood as inextricably intertwined. Mothers were well organized and politically powerful. Policies to help children were appreciated as policies that would also help and honor mothers, meaning married or widowed mothers, in an era when unwed motherhood was not defined as a major social problem. Today, in contrast, helping children invariably raises politically touchy issues of single-parent families, unwed mothers, race, and welfare.

How Can the Agenda Be Shifted?

These issues must be confronted head on because the political prospects for a New Deal for children depend heavily on shifting the agenda of American politics. The process can begin among experts and politicians, but it must eventually include voting citizens. Consensus within the elite alone will not be enough.

One part of shifting the agenda, I believe, is to replace welfare altogether with a series of more broadly constructed programs to support what I would call responsible parenting. We must carry the banner of "responsible parenting" along with "help for children" if we are to shift the political agenda.

I would like to see us combine some of the elements that Paul Starr has briefly summarized: child support assurance, job training, national health insurance, and support for families that are trying to combine work with child care. In return for its support for providing these benefits, society should accept the call of conservatives to enunciate norms of work and nurture and to impose sanctions on adults who do not comply.

Finally, any New Deal for children will depend on revitalizing a sense of civic responsibility and respect for an active public sector. Some people want to build new programs that spend more public money. Many others, some conservatives and some liberals, want new or expanded tax credits. Either way, the federal government needs a strong fiscal base. And, by itself, the end of the Cold War will not be enough to lay that base. Public faith in our public institutions and programs will have to be rekindled.

The attempt by conservatives to build a political coalition of those who are defined as producers, as opposed to beneficiaries of public programs, and to use that coalition to shrink the public sector is the most vital force in American politics now, whether one likes it or not. I don't like it, but I think we have to face it.

Helping children through public and complementary private programs that embody civic responsibility will require using politics symbolically in imaginative and constructive ways. A rational understanding of all of the reasons why children can and should be helped in cost-effective ways is not enough. We must rekindle the imagination of the American people about how our shared problems can be addressed through stronger public programs.

COMMENTS

Douglas J. Besharov

I am in broad agreement with Paul Starr's paper, although I disagree with some of the political nuances in Theda Skocpol's comments. But the devil is in the details, and I will comment on three details.

Don't Give Up on Parents

First, don't give up on parents. The most important thing for a child's development is a parent who functions well. The better the parent functions, the better the child's chances in life will be.

American parents are doing less and less for their children, whether they are middle class, rich, or poor. That is a fact, as David Hamburg describes in his paper in this volume. It is also a fact, however, that we cannot afford to replace parents.

Providing public financing for the child care paid for by parents who now work, for example, would cost $110 billion a year. Providing prenatal care and stimulating early childhood development entirely through public programs would also be extremely costly.

To improve prenatal care, the best investment would be to encourage healthy behavior in young mothers. If a young expectant mother neglects herself and her developing baby, we can spend over half a million dollars in the first six weeks of the baby's life and still have an unhappy result.

Douglas J. Besharov is a resident scholar at the American Enterprise Institute and Professor of Family Law and Policy at Georgetown University.

I am not suggesting that we turn our backs on those needful mothers. But if we want to improve the lot of neglected children, we must induce parents to change their behavior. That is true for the lower classes, the middle classes, and the upper classes alike.

Government programs cannot substitute for everything that parents do. Government strategies and spending are required; but their success means taking a very different approach to some of these issues. For example, it is many times more expensive to conduct the extensive outreach we now provide for pregnant women than it would be to provide services if the women came into public health facilities on their own.

Social Control versus Social Support

Second, the new-found concern for children could just as easily lead to more social control rather than more social support.

I started working with children many years ago as a prosecutor in New York City, handling child abuse and child neglect cases. The system of child welfare is based largely on humane concerns for children. That system today is housing almost 50,000 New York children, some in good places and some in bad, sometimes with relatives and sometimes with strangers. That is almost three times the figure of eight years ago. Today, New York City devotes 3 percent of its entire budget to housing children whom courts of law have determined have neglectful or abusive parents. Nationwide, over 410,000 children are in foster care.

Fears have already been expressed about the growth of a new paternalism, but I think we haven't seen anything yet. As government spending continues to increase, taxpayers will reevaluate the services they are providing and receiving. And there is likely to be an effort to change the behavior of people who impose costs on others, whether they be inmates of prisons or recipients of public welfare. Dealing with these pressures to use social welfare programs to "improve" the behavior of the poor, whether they come from the right or the left, will prove to be very tricky.

Health Care Costs
Are Devouring the Budget

Third, spending billions of dollars more on doctors won't help very many children.

If universal health coverage could be provided at the cost of 16 percent, 18 percent, or even 20 percent of GNP, I would sign up. But I am worried because I do not see any natural limitation on how much the country spends on health, barring major changes in philosophy and ethics.

Once I suggested establishing individual health care accounts and putting $1 million in each account. Every American, I proposed, would have a right to $1 million of health care. But no one was willing to limit the benefits to a million dollars. Some doctors spend more than that amount on an individual patient, and they will keep spending such sums unless we change our attitude toward health care. But I don't know how to do it.

In the meantime, as Paul Starr indicated, expenditures for Medicaid are displacing other expenditures. It is no accident that states are reducing AFDC payments, or not increasing them, as state expenditures for Medicaid rise. I know that much of the additional Medicaid spending is not for children, but the relationship between spending for Medicaid and AFDC is clear to budget officers nonetheless.

In conclusion, developing new policies to help children is a complicated business. Previous papers have talked about symbolism and symbolic crusades. But the debate has two sides. Each side must be very careful not to ignore the legitimate concerns of the other.

HOW MUCH DOES POVERTY MATTER?

Mary Jo Bane

I am delighted to participate in this important conference of the National Academy of Social Insurance because I am convinced that the problem of poverty among children should be viewed in the context of social insurance. To address that problem, in this paper I explore two questions: First, how does family income affect outcomes for children? Second, how much does the source of that income matter to children? I will conclude by presenting my views on how to reform welfare.

Two developments provide the context for this discussion: the trends in poverty among children and in family composition, and recent changes in welfare programs.

The Census Bureau reports that, in 1990, 20.6 percent of children under 18 lived in households with incomes below the poverty line, which was about $13,300 for a family of four in that year. The poverty rate among children reached a low of 14 percent in 1969. The rate is cyclical, and reached a high of 22.3 percent in 1983, but it also displays a trend. In 1978, a relatively good year, the poverty rate among children was 1.9 percentage points higher than it was in 1969; in 1988, it was 3.6 percentage points higher than it was in 1978.

Lying behind these figures is the growth in the number of single-parent families. About half of all children will live in a single-parent family at some point during their childhood. In 1990, the poverty rate for female-headed families with children was 44.5 percent, lower than that in 1959 (59.9 percent) but higher than that in 1979 (39.6 percent). Poor

Mary Jo Bane is commissioner of the New York State Department of Public Welfare.

female-headed families received almost half their total income from
public assistance. Most of the rest came from the mothers' own relatively
meager earnings and the earnings of others in the household; such families received virtually no child support.

These facts reflect the terrible bind in which single mothers with
low potential earnings find themselves. Most two-parent families these
days need two earners just to get by. Single-parent families, by definition, have only one potential earner, and that person is also solely
responsible for the care of the children. If she has to pay for child care, a
single parent with two children has to work full time at about $7 an hour
to lift her family above the poverty line. In most states, women with
poor education and little work experience, who cannot make that kind of
money, are better off on welfare, despite low benefits and the harassment
the welfare system imposes on recipients.

So poverty and receipt of welfare are closely intertwined for
most single-parent families. That leads to the second aspect of the context for this analysis: the alleged welfare reform efforts of states struggling with budget crises. Few states have increased AFDC benefits in
line with inflation in recent years, and some states have enacted or proposed actual benefit cuts. Others are imposing new rules and requirements on welfare recipients: requirements to work or to attend school,
penalties for additional children, and so on. The purported intent of
these proposals, besides saving money for the state, is to encourage
independence. The side effects, if the reforms are long on savings and
short on independence, may well be lower income and increased poverty
for some children.

How Much Does Income Matter?

How much difference does it really make to children, in the long
run, whether family income is lower rather than higher, and how much
difference does it make where family income comes from? The answers
to those questions may seem obvious, as they did to me about six months
ago when I started working with Larry Aber, a developmental psychol-
ogist, on a review of the literature on the effects of poverty on children.
It turns out that we do not know as much as we thought we did, or as
much as we should. But there is some exciting new research that is relevant to these issues. I will give some of the bad news first, and then some
of the good news.

The reason we think we know how poverty affects children's
development and later outcomes is that we know, both through personal
experience and from extensive data, that poor children do not do as well

as better-off children along a number of dimensions: They have more physical and mental health problems; they do not perform as well on achievement tests; they do not get as much schooling. The differences are consistent and well-documented in many reviews, notably Lorraine Klerman's study, *Alive and Well?*, prepared for the National Center for Children in Poverty.[1]

But poor children also differ from better-off children in other ways: They are much less likely to be in two-parent homes, to have parents who are well educated and employed, to go to good schools, and to live in viable communities. Asking which of these variables actually affect children's development is more than a statistician's quibble: The answer is vital in deciding whether efforts to achieve security for America's children ought to be focused on stemming welfare cuts, encouraging family financial independence, providing family services, or improving educational and health services. Even if we conclude—as is most likely—that the answer is "all of the above," it is important in these troubled fiscal times to understand which approach offers the most benefit for our dollars.

My colleagues and I have found the literature of developmental psychology to be surprisingly limited in answering these questions. Developmental psychologists understand that the development of children is related to the social and economic conditions of their families, and all the good studies control for these conditions in one way or another. But psychologists tend to believe that the social aspects of children's environment most affect their development: parent–child interaction, parental warmth, order and structure, and cognitive stimulation, among others. They believe that money is likely to affect children's development only through other aspects of the family environment. Since they have only a marginal interest in family income, family structure, education, and sources of income, they use one or a combination of these variables as controls and tend not to look systematically at their separate effects.

Most of the developmental research that we have reviewed is consistent with a conclusion that various aspects of a family's environment, including its social and economic status, affect children's cognitive and social development. But the developmentalists seem to be only beginning to explore the indirect links among family background, family interaction patterns, and child development.

Economists and other quantitative researchers have used longitudinal data to explore the links among various aspects of children's situations, including family income, and later outcomes. These studies

---

1. Klerman (1991).

lack the attention to the internal family processes and detailed structure of the home environment that developmentalists, almost surely correctly, consider so important. Nonetheless, they show some interesting findings.

Several studies have used the Panel Study of Income Dynamics, a unique twenty-year longitudinal study of over 5,000 households, to look at the effects of family background on outcomes for children. A dissertation by Naomi Goldstein at the Kennedy School is representative of these studies.[2] Goldstein looked at two outcomes, school completion and early childbearing, and a number of independent variables, including parental education, family structure, and income.

Goldstein found that parental education is by far the most important predictor of school completion. If you could change only one thing in children's lives, this would be it. We do not know exactly how it works, but many patterns are plausible: Better-educated parents provide more conversation, more reading, more motivation. Goldstein found that family income matters, too. Again, there are many plausible stories: Good income means books and toys, good care, better school environments, fewer distractions in the household.

Neither income nor education, however, was a reliable predictor of early childbearing. Instead, family structure appeared to be more important. All of this makes sense and reminds us that we are looking at extremely complicated processes.

How Much Does the Source of Income Matter?

The effects of income on children's outcomes, in the studies I just reviewed, are smaller than many people expected. Part of the reason is that other variables that are correlated with income, particularly education, appear to be more important than income by itself. But there may be another reason. Income can come from different sources, and some sources may deprive children of certain benefits even while they supply them with the benefits of more money. If, for example, the second parent in a two-parent family goes to work, family income will rise, but that parent will have less time to spend with the children. The lack of parental time or supervision, poor day care, and the stresses associated with work may affect the children adversely.

Another example comes from welfare. Welfare benefits are, of course, money, just like other income, and this money can buy food, housing, books, and other goods and services that help children's devel-

---

2. Goldstein (1991).

opment. But it is associated with, and perhaps even encourages, isolation from the economic and social mainstream, and so it may not help children as much as income from other sources.

Hill and Duncan, among others, have studied the effects of income sources on children's education and work experience.[3] They have found that the earnings of the family's head have a positive relationship to outcomes, but that welfare and the spouse's earnings have the ambiguous effects suggested by the above logic.

A study that Ginger Knox and I are doing on the effects of income and income sources on children who spent any part of their childhood in single-parent families illustrates the same points even more dramatically.[4] We used the Panel Study of Income Dynamics to examine the relationships between income from different sources during ten years of childhood and educational attainment at age 21.

Knox and I found that increases in average family income have a positive, if small, effect on children's educational attainment. We then broke our observations into two parts: We looked at the effects of income during years with two parents and during years with one parent. Though income during two-parent years had the expected positive effect, higher income during one-parent years did not seem to increase children's educational attainment. We then looked at the effects of specific income sources, with the surprising result that income from child support appeared to have strongly positive effects, whereas income from welfare and mother's earnings had ambiguous effects. These findings are not conclusive: Income from child support might be standing in for other aspects of parental interactions and family relationships that we were unable to control. But they are consistent with the view that income is not simply income: The source matters.

Another study reinforces this finding and sheds additional light on the issues before us. Nazli Baydar and Jeanne Brooks-Gunn used the National Longitudinal Surveys to search out the influences on children's scores on a cognitive test and on an index of behavioral problems.[5] The study controlled for the child's earlier scores, and thus provided a strong test of the effects of the variables of interest. Two findings are of great importance. One is that a measure called the HOME inventory was strongly predictive of cognitive skills and of behavioral problems. The HOME inventory comprises a number of dimensions of both family background, including parental warmth, and the cognitive environment. In other studies, it appears to explain much of the apparent effect of parental education and family socioeconomic status on children's devel-

---

3. Hill and Duncan (1987).
4. Knox and Bane (1991).
5. Baydar and Brooks-Gunn (1991).

opment. Even controlling for this powerful variable, however, Baydar and Brooks-Gunn found that child support improved children's development. To repeat: Income counts, largely because it can improve the home and family environment in ways that assist children; the strength of that assistance depends to some extent on the source of the money.

If these findings hold up in future research, they will have important implications for how we think about security for America's children. They are relevant to the debate about whether to provide income or services, though they do not resolve it. Some may interpret the data on the relatively weak effects of income on children's development as supporting the brief for services: Other aspects of the family environment besides income are important, so we should spend money on improving those aspects directly, through parental training, preschool education, and so on, rather than on family income support. We have to remember, however, that most of the good studies identify an income effect even after controlling for most of the things that services might affect. Moreover, the effectiveness of services is far from proven. Thus, I think we can feel safe in following our intuition that children's lives are likely to improve if their families have more money.

But the research is also beginning to suggest that the source of the money matters, and thus that some programs for increasing income may be better than others. Welfare, though necessary, is clearly not the best way to improve the lives of children. Welfare may harm children if it becomes a way of life. At the same time, an increase in income because the second parent in two-parent families goes to work, or because a single parent works more, is not an unambiguous good. The inevitable losses in parental time and the potential losses in supervision and quality of care take a toll on some children.

The only income source that seems to be unambiguously positive for children in one-parent families is child support. Unlike welfare, it is not stigmatizing or isolating. Unlike full-time work, it does not drain parental time and energy. Child support is not likely to be the sole source of support for most families. A combination of work and child support seems to be better for children than relying on maternal earnings or welfare alone, or than relying on a combination of work and welfare.

How Should Welfare Be Reformed?

This research reinforces a position that I and others have been developing over the years on the best routes to income security for that very large proportion of children who will spend part of their childhood in single-parent homes. Child support is the key, and guaranteed child support ought to be the cornerstone of government policy.

Welfare is not the answer—though punitive cuts in welfare without a substitute source of income are likely to do great harm. Recipients do not want to receive welfare, and taxpayers do not want to pay for it.

But neither is work alone the answer. Only a few single parents can do the work of two: That means working enough to earn the same as one and a half workers (the norm in two-parent families) as well as provide for child care. Single parents should not have to do the work of two; virtually every child has a second living parent.

Absent parents need to pay their fair share. Some progress has been made on that front, but much more must be done to determine paternity, establish guidelines for the size of awards, simplify procedures for obtaining awards, and withhold child support automatically from wages. In addition to enforcing child support from absent parents, the government ought to guarantee child support from public funds. Single parents need to be able to count on the regular receipt of minimum child support—enough so they can support their families with only a reasonable amount of work. I believe that the government should guarantee that minimum level of child support to every single parent. With appropriate enforcement of child support on absent parents, such a program could benefit everybody: It could reinforce family responsibility, get families off welfare and make them better off, and save money for taxpayers. It would be a genuine social insurance program, in the tradition of this country's finest efforts to ensure economic security for its citizens.

References

Bane, Mary Jo, and David T. Ellwood. "One Fifth of the Nation's Children: Why Are They Poor?" *Science*, vol. 245 (September 1989), pp. 1047–53.

Baydar, Nazli, and Jeanne Brooks-Gunn. "The Dynamics of Child Support and its Consequences for Children." Paper prepared for Conference on Child Support Reform, Airlie House, Virginia, December 1991.

Goldstein, Naomi. "Why Poverty is Bad for Children." Ph.D. dissertation. Kennedy School of Government, Harvard University, 1991.

Hill, Martha S., and Greg J. Duncan. "Parental Family Income and the Socioeconomic Attainment of Children," *Social Science Research*, vol. 16 (March 1987), pp. 39–73.

Klerman, Lorraine V. *Alive and Well? A Research and Policy Review of Health Programs for Poor Young Children.* New York: National Center for Children in Poverty, 1991.

Knox, Virginia W., and Mary Jo Bane. "The Effects of Child Support on Educational Attainment." Malcolm Wiener Center for Social Policy, 1991.

McLanahan, Sara. "Family Structure and the Reproduction of Poverty," *American Journal of Sociology,* vol. 90 (January 1985), pp. 873–901.

U.S. Bureau of the Census. Current Population Reports, Series P-60, No. 175, *Poverty in the United States: 1990.* Washington: U.S. Government Printing Office, 1991.

HOW DOES SOCIAL SECURITY PROTECT AMERICA'S CHILDREN?

Gwendolyn S. King

Several recent news stories have highlighted the plight of the nation's underprivileged children. The country's nonprofit organizations are devoting more of their energies and resources to children's issues. Within the government, the Secretary of Health and Human Services, Dr. Louis Sullivan, has created a panel that will explore public sector options for aiding America's youth. Joanne Barnhart, who heads the Administration for Children, Youth, and Families, will chair that panel, and I am very pleased to be a member of it.

One of the news stories that caught my attention quoted the head of Catholic Charities USA, telling of his frustration at not seeing more being done to help needy children. He said, "All the soup lines and shelters won't do as much for children as enlightened public policy."

This public official could not agree more with that statement. The time has come to speak loudly and bluntly about this issue. This nation has the know-how and the resourcefulness to improve our children's well-being. It is time for us to show that we have the will, the genuine desire, to take action to improve the health and welfare of our children. It is time for us to make children an urgent American priority.

Social Security is a vital component of an enlightened public policy for children. My remarks will focus on the current and future role of Social Security in the effort to help children in need, the course of our national debate on government spending priorities, and the needs of children that Social Security and other federal programs cannot address.

Gwendolyn S. King was Commissioner of Social Security.

Most of all, I want to stress the need for a widespread, intense national resolve to address these issues. At a time when American audiences are enthralled by movies like "Hook" that extol the joy and magic and unlimited horizons of childhood, wouldn't it be wonderful if we, the American people, took action on behalf of those children whose lives are devoid of magic and whose horizons do not promise cinematic happy endings?

Social Security provides a strong foundation upon which to build an effective policy for children. What I have to say about the program I administer may surprise some people. Social Security is seen by many, if not most, Americans as the institution that provides a measure of financial security to people when they reach retirement age. That is, of course, a job that Social Security has done very well for over half a century.

But the Social Security Administration (SSA) has another responsibility as well, a responsibility to millions of children who are eligible for the benefits we provide. These include children who are underprivileged and afflicted with illness or disability, children who have a parent with a disability, children who have lost a parent and now face financial despair.

When I think about my responsibility to these children, I am always deeply troubled by the statistics on poverty among the young. One in every five children under the age of eighteen is poor. Among those six and under, the ratio increases to one in every four. Among children in families headed by adults under the age of thirty—America's young families—one in every three children is in poverty. And among black children, the figures are appalling: one in two. Without Social Security, these numbers would likely be worse.

Social Security Survivors Insurance

What people don't know about Social Security is the full extent of what it does for children and families. In December 1991, the Social Security Administration, through its old-age, survivors, and disability insurance (OASDI) program provided over $1 billion in benefits to over 3 million children. That's nearly as much money as the aid to families with dependent children program provides to children in a typical month. Social Security, in other words, is a crucial if relatively quiet component of the public sector effort to aid children.

Survivors insurance is probably the most overlooked portion of Social Security. Survivors insurance reflects the philosophy that the unexpected death of a family breadwinner should not be accompanied by financial tragedy as well. Survivors benefits help cushion the blow for these families, giving them the chance to recover and get back on their feet.

Of the 40 million people receiving OASDI benefits, over 7 million are receiving survivors benefits. That includes 1.8 million children. Coverage under this program is extremely widespread. Right now, 98 of every 100 children could get benefits if a working parent should die.

A little realized fact about the survivors insurance program is that it offers, for families and children, a greater value than most commercial life insurance policies. The protection for families through OASDI survivors benefits is equivalent to a life insurance policy with a face value of $85,000. Because OASDI benefits vary according to the structure of the family, the value of that protection could be as high as $390,000 for young families with two or more children. The total survivors protection offered to all children is currently estimated to be about $7.6 trillion.

Under the current rules, survivors benefits can be paid to unmarried children under 18, or 19 if they are attending secondary school full-time. They are also paid to those who were disabled before the age of 22 and remain disabled. Social Security currently pays benefits to more than 600,000 people who were disabled before the age of 18 and were children of retired, disabled, or deceased workers.

Although survivors insurance is the primary means by which children receive benefits under Social Security, it is not the only one. In December 1991, we delivered checks to just over 1 million children who have a disabled worker as a parent. And we sent benefits to over 400,000 children of older parents who are now retired. All in all, through the OASDI program, we have an effective safety net that, to a great degree, protects America's children from the financial effects of their parents' death, disability, or retirement.

Supplemental Security Income

Still another publicly funded program assists our neediest children. Supplemental security income (SSI) provides benefits to people who are aged, blind, or disabled and have little or no income or assets. Children who are from needy families and who have a disability may be eligible for SSI benefits.

There is good and bad news here. SSI is important because it gives us a tool to address the special needs of these children. With the benefits SSI provides, children with disabilities who are poor can receive dollars to use for food, clothing, or housing. More important, SSI benefits are a key to doors to much-needed health benefits. Eligibility for SSI leads to eligibility for other government programs. That is the good news.

The bad news is that these children, these potential beneficiaries, are among the most difficult for us to find and help. Throughout the history of SSI, the government has not been successful in delivering benefits to all of the citizens who are potential recipients. That is particularly true with potentially eligible children, who are difficult to identify and locate and difficult to reach with information about the SSI program.

Homelessness intensifies that problem. According to the 1990 report of the U.S. Conference of Mayors, families with children make up 34 percent of the urban homeless.[1] Whatever the numbers, the fact that confronts us is that many of the nation's children who could be benefiting from SSI dollars—either on their own account or on their parents'— have no fixed address and, thus, are very difficult to locate and assist.

Let me make my feelings and my policy on this matter very clear. We have a responsibility to every one of these children who are eligible for benefits, whether or not they have an address. I will never accept an America in which children needing help from their government, eligible for help from their government, grow up in despair and receive no helping hand. That is not the America I know.

Outreach Efforts

Outreach is a major priority for the Social Security Administration. By developing more aggressive public information programs, by sending our employees into the shelters and the soup kitchens, by building coalitions with interest groups and community organizations for the single purpose of helping needy children, we are making progress.

But each of us involved with this issue, in and out of government, must come to grips with a disquieting fact: Only a limited number of organizations and individuals are willing to put their time and their sweat and their resources into this crusade. Between the government and many of these groups, and between the groups themselves, lie long histories of differences and conflict. We must put aside those differences, recognize the importance of working together, and join hands to get this job done.

Our coalition building is paying off. In December 1989, just over 296,000 children who were blind or who had a disability were receiving federal benefits. By the end of 1991, nearly 439,000 children were receiv-

---

1. DeIulio (1991).

ing those benefits. That's a 48 percent increase in just twenty-four months. Some of that increase, admittedly, is due to the slow growth of the economy. Much of it, however, is due to our getting the word out and finding the people, the children, who need our help.

Today we are experiencing unprecedented growth in the number of children served by our disability program. It is the fastest growing category within SSI, both in number of claims filed and in claims allowed. Those numbers will continue to rise because of two noteworthy developments.

Children with AIDS

First, we have recently added special guidelines to identify disability in children with HIV infection and children with AIDS. These new guidelines recognize the fact that younger children with HIV infection can differ from adults, or even from older children, in the ways they have become infected and in the course of their disease.

SSA recognizes that some children may not appear to have the exact conditions specified in the written guidelines. But they may have other signs and symptoms indicative of HIV infection that affect their ability to grow, develop, or engage in activities similar to those of well children of the same age. We have established a policy that is both flexible and compassionate, enabling us to aid children afflicted with this tragic disease.

Revised Disability Criteria

The other development that will spur the expansion of the childhood disability program arises from the largest class action judgment ever implemented by the Social Security Administration. It involves a massive effort to locate children who were denied benefits from 1980 to 1991 and who, under revised disability criteria, may very well be eligible today for current and retroactive benefits.

Last year, we sent notices to more than 450,000 children who were denied benefits under the old regulations, offering them the opportunity to bring their cases back to SSA for reexamination and a new determination. So far, about 200,000 children and families have responded, and we are processing their new claims. I expect to complete review of the class members by the end of 1992. My goal has always been to make certain that these children wait no longer for the benefits that they should already have been receiving.

I hope I have illustrated the extremely high priority that all 66,000 employees of the Social Security Administration assign to America's most vulnerable children. Through Social Security and supplemental security income, we are delivering critical financial benefits to nearly 3 million children who might otherwise be living lives without any hope. We will continue our outreach efforts to find more children in this country who are eligible for assistance but are not yet receiving it.

Where Do We Go from Here?

The question remains, then, where do we go from here? What do we, as policymakers and as policy analysts and scholars, do, from this day forward, to help America's children? What can I—as Social Security commissioner and as a citizen concerned about our nation's future— advocate to keep this national discussion moving in a productive, forward direction?

Generational Issues

I have a couple of lines of thought. The first concerns Social Security and other federal benefit programs and the current national debate over government spending priorities.

Social Security, as I have explained, is among the government's most important programs in providing financial protection and security to our nation's children. It is, therefore, incumbent upon future Presidents and Congresses, upon those of you who have strong and influential voices in determining the future of Social Security, to work to maintain a program that is as effective and as secure as it is today.

In many circles it is trendy to cast the discussion about the welfare of children as an intergenerational struggle. Each of us has seen the figures quoted many times—the far greater amount of public funds spent on the elderly than on children. Each of has heard the inflammatory rhetoric about "greedy geezers" snatching resources from defenseless babes. These are issues that stir emotional, even incendiary, debate. One has to question, however, the relevance of those statistics, given the different circumstances and challenges affecting the lives of children and the elderly. And one has to question the usage of that rhetoric if its real purpose is to undermine public support for vital programs like Social Security.

It is an ugly thought, this idea of children and their grandparents at each other's throats for the same piece of the public pie. And it is a battle that is wholly undesirable and wholly unnecessary.

I subscribe instead to a passage penned by Pearl Buck. She wrote, "I do not believe in a child world. I believe the child should be taught from the very first that the whole world is his world, and that adult and child share one world, that all generations are needed."

Who says our national policy cannot recognize, equally, the needs of the vulnerable elderly and of the vulnerable young? Who says that programs for the elderly and programs for children must be pitted against each other, with one gaining only if the other loses? Who has decided that federal dollars are the prize in a tug-of-war between old and young?

Those who advocate a public policy in which one generation must suffer for another to be better protected are not leading America in the right direction. We need to do a better job of articulating a public policy for a stronger, healthier America. We need to look at all programs, all initiatives, our entire domestic policy and determine how our dollars can best be spent for the greatest good of those with the greatest needs.

Nonmonetary Issues

That leads to my second line of thought: We cannot afford to look at the needs of our nation's children as needs that can be addressed solely through the dollars provided by federal benefit programs. This volume is dedicated to security for America's children, and I believe that the challenge of achieving that security is too broad and too complex to be met with money alone.

A striking study that was published recently in *Science*, performed by researchers from Stanford and from the National Bureau of Economic Research, showed a decline in the well-being and performance of children over the last three years despite a rise in government spending on programs that benefit children.[2] This study revealed that, between 1960 and 1988, student test scores have dropped, teen suicide rates have tripled, and teen homicide rates have tripled as well, a rate of increase that exceeds that for adults.

Other studies tell the same story. Teenage birth rates, for example, have exploded. In 1988, over 20,000 teenagers gave birth not to their first, not just to their second, but to their third child.[3] Not only do those teenage mothers face lives of great difficulty, but so, tragically, does an entire generation of children, who will have little chance of escaping the cycle of poverty they have entered at birth.

---

2. Fuchs and Reklis (1992).
3. National Center for Health Statistics (1991).

We cannot repair the damage being done to our nation's children through benefit programs alone. I am proud of the program we are administering at the Social Security Administration. I am proud of what we are doing to funnel those benefits to more eligible kids. But I realize that, even if we poured millions more dollars into those programs, they are not going to remedy every problem that our children face. Governments, schools, businesses, communities, and individuals who care must adjust to today's realities. And, within those limits, we must work together to make things better.

Employers, for example, in this day of two-earner and single-parent households, need to recognize the importance of on-site child care, of flexible hours, of work-at-home options, and so enable their employees to be both productive professionals and nurturing parents. The Social Security Administration is pursuing and implementing those policies. We have, for example, installed child care facilities in two of our largest installations—our central office at Woodlawn and our processing center in downtown Baltimore. The Baltimore facility, we were pleased to learn, has been named a winner of the Presidential Federal Design Achievement Award.

Schools, churches, communities—all of us—need to work together to reach out to children who are without guidance, without direction, and without a compelling reason to go to school, to study hard, to work to improve themselves and their prospects in life. The Social Security Administration, to cite another example with which I am very familiar, has an adopt-a-school program, linking our employees with Baltimore school-age children in a variety of activities.

Social Security, by doing what it is doing through its benefit programs, can address only one dimension of this issue. Bringing better, more promising lives to our nation's young people requires broad, multidimensional thinking. The National Academy of Social Insurance is one organization that has chosen to take on this difficult, yet essential, task. We pledge to work closely with you in the weeks and months ahead to develop new ideas, to forge new directions, and to strengthen our mutual resolve to help America's children.

References

DeIulio, John J. "There But for Fortune—The Homeless: Who They Are and How to Help Them," *New Republic,* vol. 204 (June 24, 1991), pp. 27–36.

Fuchs, Victor R., and D.M. Reklis. "America's Children: Economic Perspectives and Policy Options," *Science*, vol. 255 (January 3, 1992), pp. 41–46.

National Center for Health Statistics. Telephone interview. December 1991.

PART II

---●◉●---

RETOOLING FOR
CHILDREN'S INCOME SECURITY

CHILD SUPPORT ASSURANCE: AN ADDITION TO OUR SOCIAL SECURITY MENU

Irwin Garfinkel

We are not doing a very good job of providing security for America's children. The situation for children living with single mothers is particularly grim. Nearly half of these children are poor. And the more fortunate half experience the insecurity that arises from the sudden large drops in income that accompany divorce. These income drops average 50 percent. What's more, demographers tell us, one half of all children in this generation will spend part of their childhood living with a single mother.

Why does our Social Security system do so little to reduce this virulent form of insecurity? In 1935, at the time of the Social Security Act, most single mothers were widows and they were not expected to work. Now most single mothers are divorced, separated, or never married. Since the revolutionary increases in the labor force participation of married women, single mothers have been expected to work. Social Security, like any successful social institution, is slow to adapt to change. As a consequence, although survivors insurance does a good job of reducing insecurity and preventing poverty and welfare dependence among widows and their children, the only protection afforded to children living with divorced, separated, and never married mothers is welfare. But welfare helps only those who have fallen into poverty. It does

---

Irwin Garfinkel is a professor of social work at Columbia University.

nothing to prevent poverty. Moreover, welfare is a substitute for, rather than a supplement to earnings. Welfare cannot help make work pay. To reduce insecurity, prevent poverty, and make work pay, the nation should add to its menu of Social Security programs a new child support assurance system.

A child support assurance system, or as David Ellwood likes to call it, a child support enforcement and insurance system, is easy to explain. To be eligible to participate in the system, a child would have to be legally entitled to receive private child support from a parent living apart from the child. The amount of private support owed by the nonresident parent would be a percentage of his or her income that depended upon the number of children owed support. The resulting obligation would be routinely withheld from wages and other sources of income just like income and payroll taxes. Finally, the child's caretaker would receive either what the nonresident parent pays or an assured child support benefit, whichever is higher. When nonresident parents paid less than the assured child support benefit level, the government would make up the difference.

Child support assurance is patterned after survivors insurance. Like survivors insurance, it aids children of all income classes who suffer an income loss due to the absence of a parent. Survivors insurance compensates for the loss of income arising from widowhood; child support assurance would compensate for the loss arising from divorce, separation, and nonmarriage. The percentage-of-income standard in conjunction with routine income withholding makes the bulk of the financing of child support assurance similar to a proportional payroll tax, which is used to finance all of our social insurance programs. In the case of child support assurance, however, the tax applies only to those who are legally liable for child support. The assured-benefit component of child support assurance makes the benefit structure like that of other social insurance programs in that it provides greater benefits to low-income families than are justified on the basis of the family's contributions or taxes.

Finally, a child support assurance system, like Social Security and universal elementary and secondary education, is designed to prevent poverty and welfare dependence. Welfare programs relieve poverty; Social Security and free public education prevent it. It is constructive in this context to examine the views of the architects of our Social Security system. They believed that it was the obligation of the government both to provide relief to people who needed it and to prevent as many people as possible from needing it. Despite the fact that the architects of the Social Security Act provided federal cash relief on an unprecedented scale and enacted three new permanent federal cash relief programs—aid to the aged and blind as well as aid to dependent children—they remained uncomfortable with the widespread provision of cash relief, even for persons not expected to work. Indeed, President Franklin Delano Roosevelt referred to cash relief as a narcotic.[1] Even though poor widows and their children were already eligible for aid to dependent children, the architects of our Social Security system advocated the creation of a survivors insurance program. Their strong preference for preventing rather than relieving poverty is evident in the following excerpt from the report of the 1938 Advisory Council on Social Security:

> While public assistance is now being provided to a large number of dependent children in this country on a needs-test basis, the arguments for substituting benefits as a matter of right in the case of children are even more convincing than in the case of aged persons. A democratic society has an immeasurable stake in avoiding the growth of a habit of dependence among its youth. The method of survivors' insurance not only sustains the concept that a child is supported through the efforts of the parent but affords a vital sense of security to the family unit.[2]

If the architects of the Social Security Act could invent a social institution that assured that children were supported by their deceased parents, surely we can invent a social institution to assure that children are supported by their living parents.

Child support assurance differs from social insurance in one respect. In social insurance programs, contributions typically take place before the event requiring the insurance. In the child support assurance system (CSAS), the nonresident parent pays child support only after becoming a nonresident parent. That is why its advocates in Wisconsin chose the name assurance rather than insurance. In the rest of this paper, I describe the weaknesses of the old system and the evolution toward a new child support assurance system. Then I address the following questions: What are the advantages of child support assurance? How does it differ from welfare? How much will it cost, and how much will it contribute to making work pay, as reflected in reductions in poverty and in welfare caseloads? Finally, I will comment briefly on where we should go from here.

---

1. Brown (1940).
2. Advisory Council on Social Security (1938), pp. 192-93.

Weaknesses of the Old
Child Support Assurance System
and Evolution toward a New System

Before 1975, child support was almost exclusively a state and local matter. State laws established the duty of nonresident parents to pay child support but left all the details up to local courts.[3] Judges decided whether any child support should be paid and, if so, how much. They also had full authority over what to do if the nonresident parent failed to pay.

The old child support system condoned and therefore fostered parental irresponsibility. Only six of ten mothers who were potentially eligible for it were awarded child support. Among mothers with legal awards, only half received the full amount to which they were entitled, and over a quarter received nothing. The system was rife with inequity. Child support awards for children and parents in similar economic circumstances varied widely.[4] While most nonresident fathers paid no child support and suffered no consequences, thousands of others were sent to jail. Poor nonresident fathers who were legally obligated to pay child support were required to pay substantially higher proportions of their incomes than middle-income nonresident fathers.[5] Finally, nearly half of single mothers and their children were poor and dependent on welfare.[6]

Critics of the old system suggested many reforms. The common element of virtually all of these suggestions was the replacement of judicial discretion with the bureaucratic regularity characteristic of our social insurance and income tax systems. This tendency is clearly articulated in the proposal to add to our menu of Social Security programs a new child support assurance system.[7]

It is remarkable how far the country has moved in the last seven years toward such a system. The Child Support Enforcement Amendments of 1984 required states to adopt numeric child support guidelines that courts could use to determine child support obligations; and it required them to withhold child support obligations from wages and other income of nonresident parents who become delinquent in their

---

3. For the best single description, see Krause (1981); for flavor, see Chambers (1979); for numbers, see Cassetty (1978).
4. White and Stone (1976), p.83; Yee (1979), p.21.
5. Cassetty (1978); Garfinkel and Melli (1982).
6. Garfinkel and McLanahan (1986).
7. Wisconsin Department of Health and Social Services (1979); Garfinkel and Melli (1982).

payment of child support for one month. The 1984 act also took a step, if an extremely cautious one, in the direction of assuring a minimum child support benefit; it directed the Secretary of Health and Human Services (HHS) to allow Wisconsin to use federal AFDC monies to help fund an assured child support benefit.

The Family Support Act of 1988 strengthened the 1984 guidelines and withholding provisions. Whereas the 1984 amendments allowed the courts to ignore the guidelines, the 1988 legislation makes the guidelines the presumptive child support award. Judges may depart from the guidelines only if they write a justification that can be reviewed by a higher court. Furthermore, the Family Support Act requires that, starting in 1993, states review and update child support awards for families receiving child support enforcement services under Title IV-D of the Social Security Act at least every three years, and it directs the Secretary of HHS to study the impact of requiring periodic reviews of all child support cases. The 1988 legislation also required routine withholding of the child support obligation for all cases under Title IV-D as of 1990, and for all child support cases as of 1994. Finally, the Congress granted New York a waiver similar to Wisconsin's to use federal AFDC funds to undertake a pilot program for an assured child support benefit.

The Advantages of a New Child Support Assurance System

The new child support assurance system has a number of advantages over the traditional system. All three of its components—the guidelines, the routine withholding of payments from income, and the assured benefit—will increase the incomes of eligible families and thereby help make work pay. Unlike welfare, income from CSAS will not be reduced as earnings increase. Therefore, CSAS will supplement rather than replace earnings.

If child support obligations were equal to 17 percent of gross income for one child, and 25 percent, 29 percent, 31 percent, and 34 percent respectively for two, three, four, and five or more children—which are the percentages adopted by Wisconsin—child support payments would increase more than $6 billion. Making the child support obligation equal to a percentage of the nonresident parent's income will also reduce inequities and improve understanding of the system. It will provide automatic indexing of child support awards, so that as the income of the nonresident parent increases, the amount owed will automatically rise. Similarly, if the earnings of a nonresident parent decrease because of unemployment or illness, the child support obligation will automatically drop.

Routine withholding from income increases both the size and timeliness of child support payments. Nonresident parents who have defaulted for a few months may have spent the money for other purposes and often cannot afford to pay back the arrearage. During the early 1980s, when Wisconsin had a law requiring withholding in response to delinquency, 70 percent of nonresident parents became delinquent within three years.[8] No society profits by creating so many lawbreakers. Routine withholding of child support obligations from income is a preventive measure that removes stigma and punishment from the collection process while enhancing children's economic security.

Because the nation has taken only the most limited steps toward an assured child support benefit, I will devote more attention to its advantages. The assured benefit insures children from middle- and upper-income families against the risk that their nonresident parent will fail to pay child support. Sudden declines in the nonresident parent's income now frequently result in a precipitous decline in child support. An assured benefit would cushion this fall.

The assured benefit also opens a door out of poverty for those whose earnings ability and child support entitlements are low. In the absence of an assured benefit, a large proportion of welfare mothers would still be poor even if they worked full time and received all the private child support to which they were entitled. The assured benefit will encourage work and reduce welfare dependence. Unlike welfare, the assured benefit will not be reduced by one dollar for each dollar of earnings.

In other words, an assured child support benefit will reduce economic insecurity and dependence on welfare simultaneously. Private child support is irregular. An assured benefit provides a secure base of child support. That is of value to single mothers from all income classes, but it is particularly valuable for single mothers with low earnings capacity. For them, it makes life outside welfare far more tolerable. In short, an assured benefit makes work pay.

If dependence on welfare is of no concern, it is easy to increase economic security. Just make welfare benefits more generous. That is exactly what happened between 1955 and 1975; not surprisingly, the proportion of single mothers dependent on welfare went from under 40 percent to over 60 percent.[9] Conversely, if the economic security of single mothers and their children is of no concern, it is easy to reduce welfare

---

8. The estimate is based on data from court records in twenty Wisconsin counties.

9. Moffitt (1990) reports that caseloads were equal to only 36 percent in 1967 and 62 percent by 1975.

rolls. Just cut benefits. That is what has been done since 1975; welfare rolls have dropped from over 60 percent to about 45 percent of single mothers. What the nation needs now are policies that reduce both insecurity and dependence. That's why an assured benefit is so attractive.

Finally, the assured benefit will be an effective means of reinvesting the savings that will arise from increases in child support collections for children now dependent on welfare. Sharing the gains of reductions in welfare costs with poor families who have child support awards not only bolsters their incomes in times of hardship, but also gives mothers who want to make a life outside of welfare a concrete reason for determining paternity. By the same token it gives welfare officials and community activists a tool in their efforts to reduce both welfare caseloads and economic insecurity.

Strengthening child support enforcement has already begun to reduce the costs of aid to families with dependent children and will do so even more in the future.[10] The savings in AFDC could be used to reduce taxes, but inasmuch as children potentially eligible for child support and the mothers who care for them are among our poorest citizens, using these funds to provide an assured benefit is the compassionate thing to do. Because half of the next generation will be potentially eligible for child support, it is also a wise investment in our future.

Is an Assured Benefit Just Welfare by Another Name?

Perhaps the most frequent criticism of an assured child support benefit is that it is just welfare by another name. Of course, both an assured benefit and welfare are public transfers. But it is important to distinguish between public transfers that are income tested (like welfare) and those that are not (like Social Security). The differences between what are conventionally called welfare programs, such as AFDC and food stamps, and universal programs, such as old-age insurance and the proposed assured child support benefit, are profound. This is not mere semantics. To say that the assured benefit is just welfare by another name is equivalent to saying that apples are just oranges because apples and oranges are both fruit.

The assured benefit differs from AFDC in a myriad of ways. Unlike AFDC, an assured child support benefit makes eligibility dependent upon legal entitlement to receive private child support rather than

---

10. Child support payments for children on AFDC have increased from $0.2 billion in 1976 to $1.5 billion in 1988. See U.S. Department of Health and Human Services (various years).

upon income. The program is not for the poor alone but for children with nonresident parents from all income classes. Because its benefits are limited to the poor, AFDC contains strong disincentives against work and remarriage. It isolates its beneficiaries from the social mainstream by funneling them through a separate bureaucracy—which, moreover, is expensive to administer. It stigmatizes them. AFDC provides no help whatsoever to the millions of single mothers and children who are economically insecure though not abjectly impoverished. A universal assured child support benefit will encourage poor mothers now mired within welfare to work and remarry. It will integrate these women and their children into the social mainstream. Unlike welfare, the child support assurance system will be cheap to administer and will treat its beneficiaries with dignity. Finally, unlike welfare, but like Social Security, CSAS will increase the economic security of all children potentially eligible for child support.

In short, to those who say an assured benefit is just welfare by another name, my response is twofold. First, the differences are legion and fundamental. Second, why argue semantics? Even if an assured child support benefit were just welfare by another name, would not the critical question be whether it is a better form of welfare than what we have now?

Costs and Benefits of a Child Support Assurance System

The first question that policymakers ask about the child support assurance system is, How much will it cost? A second question is, What are the benefits. And a third is, To what extent will CSAS make work pay?

In collaboration with others, I have developed a microsimulation model to estimate the costs and benefits of CSAS.[11] Reductions in poverty and AFDC caseloads are used to measure both the benefits of CSAS and the extent to which CSAS makes work pay. Table 1 presents estimates of costs (or savings) and reductions in poverty and AFDC caseloads for national child support assurance programs of different degrees of generosity and different degrees of effectiveness of child support collections.

The estimates in the top panel of table 1 assume that the collection system is 100 percent effective. That is, there are child support

---

11. For a description of the microsimulation model used to derive these estimates, see Garfinkel and others (1990), pp. 1–31.

awards in all cases, the awards are equal to the Wisconsin standard as a percentage of income, and all of the awards are paid in full.

The first row of the panel presents estimates in which there is no assured benefit. The next three rows present estimates in which the assured benefit level for the first child equals $1,000, $2,000, and $3,000.[12] (In all cases, assured benefits are assumed to be $1,000 each for the second and third child and $500 each for the fourth, fifth, and sixth child.)

Only the most generous benefit of $3,000 for the first child costs money. The savings for the less generous assured benefits arise because the extra dollars paid out under the new system will be more than offset by increases in child support collections and consequent reductions in welfare expenditures.

For families eligible for child support, the reductions in the poverty gap—which is measured as the funds needed to bridge the gap between the poverty line and a family's current income— are substantial. Even with no assured benefit, increases in child support collections would narrow the poverty gap nearly one-quarter. Adding the assured benefit of $3,000 for the first child nearly doubles the reduction in poverty—from 24 percent to 40 percent. Similarly, reductions in welfare caseloads are very large, ranging from a low of 20 percent in the absence of an assured child support benefit to 49 percent with an assured benefit of $3,000.[13]

As already noted, the estimates in the top panel of table 1 assume a perfect system of child support collections. As of 1991, however, the system was a long way from perfection. Enactment of a child support assurance system will increase the proportion of cases with child support awards, the average level of awards, and the proportion of awards that are paid. What we do not know now is how much and how fast. Thus, the estimates in the top panel should be interpreted as lower bounds on the long-run costs and upper bounds of the long-run effects of CSAS on reductions in poverty and welfare dependence.

The second panel in table 1 presents short-run lower-bound estimates of the benefits and short-run upper-bound estimates of the costs of CSAS. These estimates assume no increase in child support award rates, award levels, or payment rates. Because all three are expected to increase, these assumptions underestimate benefits and overestimate costs.

---

12. The public-subsidy portion of the assured benefit is taxable income for the resident parent and the federal revenue derived from making it taxable is subtracted from the estimated cost of the assured benefit.

13. The estimates of reductions in welfare caseload may be too high or too low because they are based on annual data, whereas eligibility is based on monthly income.

Table 1
Estimated Benefits and Costs of a
National Child Support Assurance System

Assured benefit level[1] (1985 dollars)	Reduction in poverty gap[2] (percent)	Reduction in AFDC cases (percent)	Net cost (billions of 1985 dollars)
	Perfect system[3]		
None	24	20	−2.7
1,000	25	23	−2.5
2,000	30	33	−1.4
3,000	40	49	0.7
	Short run I[4]		
None	0	0	0
1,000	2	3	0.5
2,000	5	8	2.1
3,000	9	14	4.7
	Short run II[5]		
None	2	2	−0.1
1,000	3	4	0.1
2,000	5	8	0.9
3,000	9	14	2.7
	Intermediate run[6]		
None	12	9	−1.1
1,000	13	12	−0.8
2,000	17	20	0.1
3,000	24	32	2.1

Source: Author's calculations. For a description of the model, see Garfinkel and others (1990).

1. For the first child. The assured benefits are assumed to be $1,000 each for the second and third child and $500 each for the fourth, fifth, and sixth child.

2. The poverty gap is measured as the funds needed to bridge the gap between the poverty line and a family's current income.

3. Awards are made in all cases; awards are set at Wisconsin standard; all awards are paid in full.

4. No increase from current levels in award rates or levels, or in payment rates.

5. Same as short-run I except that awards are set at Wisconsin standard.

6. Award rates and collection rates are halfway between current levels and perfection; awards are set at Wisconsin standard.

The short-run benefits of CSAS are quite modest. An assured benefit of $2,000 shaves only 5 percent from the poverty gap and only 8 percent from AFDC caseloads. Even the assured benefit of $3,000 for the first child reduces the gap only 9 percent and caseloads by just 14 percent. These are not trivial effects, but they are only one-quarter of the upper-bound estimates of long-run benefits. Furthermore, in the short run, with no improvements in child support enforcement, CSAS would cost from $0.5 billion to $4.7 billion.

These net costs can be reduced substantially and immediately by restricting eligibility to children whose awards have been updated to the Wisconsin standard. This single improvement, as the third panel of table 1 indicates, will cut costs to virtually zero for a $1,000 assured benefit, and to $0.9 billion and $2.7 billion for the $2,000 and $3,000 assured benefit levels respectively. Awareness of these differences between the short- and long-run benefits and costs of CSAS led the architects of the Wisconsin system to recommend that it be enacted in stages, beginning with the reforms in collection procedures. The country as a whole has, in fact, already taken giant strides toward CSAS on the collection side.

Finally, it is worth emphasizing that as long as eligibility is limited to families with new or updated child support awards, the cost of a $1,000 assured child support benefit is practically zero, even in the short run. Even the cost of a $2,000 assured benefit is less than $1 billion. Therefore, we could enact a very small assured child support benefit and get started down the right path at practically no cost.

The bottom panel in table 1 presents some intermediate-run estimates of the benefits and costs of CSAS. Both award rates and collection rates are halfway between their current levels and perfection. All awards are assumed to be equal to the Wisconsin standard.

The costs are small. An assured benefit of $2,000 costs almost nothing. Even an assured benefit of $3,000 costs only $2 billion. Moreover, the benefits are fairly large. With an assured benefit of $2,000, both the poverty gap and AFDC caseloads shrink almost 20 percent. A $3,000 benefit shrinks the poverty gap 24 percent and AFDC caseloads 32 percent.

The estimates suggest that a new child support assurance system represents a marked improvement over the old system. Therefore it is not surprising that the country is in the process of abandoning the old and moving toward the new system.

The estimates also highlight the limitations of a child support assurance in reducing economic insecurity and welfare dependence. While noteworthy and worth achieving, a one-fifth reduction in poverty and welfare dependence still leaves 80 percent of both problems. Even if the private child support system worked to perfection, 60 percent of the poverty gap and over half of the AFDC caseload would remain. Other policies that simultaneously reduce insecurity and welfare dependence are needed to complement child support assurance.[14]

A Full-Fledged Child Support Assurance System?

Although the nation is in the process of adopting a child support assurance system, we have not completed the task. Despite the adoption of guidelines, the courts, rather than being reserved for rare appeals, are still heavily involved in determining the child support obligation. Few states have implemented universal, routine withholding of child support obligations. All states are a long way from universal establishment of paternity. And perhaps most important, neither the federal government nor any state has adopted an assured child support benefit.

In concluding, I want to emphasize the close relationship between the establishment of paternity and the adoption of an assured child support benefit. The assured benefit fosters the establishment of paternity. To qualify for an assured child support benefit, mothers of children born out of wedlock will have to identify the fathers of their children.

At the same time, the extent to which the assured benefit reduces economic insecurity and welfare dependence depends critically on the extent to which it fosters the establishment of paternity. Thus the adoption of the system is also likely to induce community leaders to urge the poor to be more cooperative in establishing paternity. Historically, these advocates have not looked upon child support enforcement with much enthusiasm. This is understandable: In the presence of AFDC and the absence of an assured benefit, child support enforcement is Robin Hood in reverse—taking from poor fathers to reduce AFDC costs and the tax burden of middle- and upper-income families. If one believes, as I do, that poor fathers should be paying child support, enforcement is hardly equivalent to stealing. Nevertheless, strengthening enforcement does redistribute from poor to rich. An assured benefit has the reverse effect.[15] It reinvests the AFDC savings in poor families—provided that these families establish paternity and entitlement to child support and earn enough to leave welfare.

---

14. For discussion of such policies see Garfinkel and McLanahan (1986), Ellwood (1988), and Kamerman and Kahn (1988).

15. Some families who would never have been on welfare will also benefit from CSAS and to that extent, an assured benefit by itself cannot eliminate all the reverse redistribution.

Thus child support assurance may be viewed as a three-legged stool, whose balance relies as much on the assured benefit as on numerical guidelines for payments and routine withholding of payments from income.

References

Advisory Council on Social Security. *Final Report.* December 10, 1938. In *The Report of the Committee on Economic Security of 1935, Fiftieth Anniversary Edition.* Washington: National Conference on Social Welfare, 1985.

Brown, Josephine C. *Public Relief 1929–1939.* New York: Henry Holt and Co., 1940.

Cassetty, Judith. *Child Support and Public Policy: Securing Support from Absent Fathers.* Lexington: D.C. Heath, 1978.

Chambers, David. *Making Fathers Pay: The Enforcement of Child Support.* Chicago: University of Chicago Press, 1979.

Ellwood, David T. *Poor Support: Poverty in the American Family.* New York: Basic Books, 1988.

Garfinkel, Irwin, and Sara S. McLanahan. *Single Mothers and Their Children: A New American Dream.* Washington: Urban Institute Press, 1986.

_____, and Marygold Melli. "Child Support: Weaknesses of the Old and Features of a Proposed New System." Institute for Research on Poverty Special Report No. 32A. Madison: University of Wisconsin, 1982.

_____, and others. "The Wisconsin Child Support Assurance System: Estimated Effects on Poverty, Labor Supply, Caseloads, and Costs," *Journal of Human Resources,* vol. 25 (winter 1990), pp. 1–31.

Kamerman, Sheila B., and Alfred J. Kahn. *Mothers Alone: Strategies for a Time of Change.* Dover, MA: Auburn House Publishing Company, 1988.

Krause, Harry O. *Child Support in America: The Legal Perspective.* Charlottesville: Michie, 1981.

Moffitt, Robert. "Incentive Effects of the U.S. Welfare System: A Review." Institute for Research on Poverty Special Report No. 48. Madison: University of Wisconsin, 1990.

U.S. Department of Health and Human Services, Office of Child Support Enforcement. *Child Support Enforcement, Annual Report to Congress.* Washington: Government Printing Office, annual.

White, Kenneth R., and R. Thomas Stone. "A Study of Alimony and Child Support Rulings with Some Recommendations," *Family Law Quarterly*, vol. 10 (spring 1976), pp. 75–91.

Wisconsin Department of Health and Social Services. "Wisconsin Welfare Study 1978: Report and Recommendations of the Welfare Reform Study Advisory Committee." 1979.

Yee, L.M. "What Really Happens in Child Support Cases: An Empirical Study of the Establishment and Enforcement of Child Support in the Denver District Court," *Denver Law Journal*, vol. 57 (1979, no. 1), pp. 21–70.

MAKING WORK PAY

Judith M. Gueron

The nation's struggle to design social welfare policy has reflected a continuing effort to meet two distinct objectives: reducing poverty among children and encouraging work and self-support by their parents. Unfortunately, we have learned over the years that more of one can mean less of the other. This quandary flows in part from our heavy reliance on means-tested programs. By their very design, such programs discourage work, since benefits are reduced as income grows. And the more seriously we take their antipoverty goal, the more generous we make the programs, the more we risk undermining self-reliance and blunting the incentive for welfare recipients to take low-paying jobs. Yet, as proposals in this country shift toward universal programs, we should remember why we have relied on means-tested programs so heavily in the past: They embody an effort to contain costs, target scarce resources on the most disadvantaged, and get the most antipoverty payoff for any particular outlay.

Henry Aaron recently observed that this country is particularly concerned with the behavioral effects of government programs, especially with the extent to which generous cash transfers reduce labor supply. Although this tradeoff between program goals has been evident for years, because of this effect we seem to be paralyzed by the choices. The outcome is that we stumble in our attempt both to combat poverty and to increase self-sufficiency and that we continue to seek reforms—both incremental and fundamental—that can improve our performance in one

Judith M. Gueron is president of the Manpower Demonstration Research Corporation.

direction without sacrificing too much in the other, and thereby bring the system more nearly in balance with underlying public values.

In this paper, I will focus on what we know about encouraging work among single mothers in the aid to families with dependent children (AFDC) program. I do not usually start with anecdotes; the business of the Manpower Demonstration Research Corporation (MDRC), after all, is conducting large-scale, rigorous studies of the effectiveness of social programs. But this tradeoff was brought home to me recently by the experience of one young woman in just such a study. MDRC is in the midst of a sixteen-site demonstration of New Chance, a comprehensive program of education, training, and personal development services for teenage mothers on welfare and their children. The goal is self-sufficiency for the mothers and improved outcomes for their children. Recently, the program director at a site in a state with relatively low welfare grants recounted the dilemma facing a participant who had just completed the program. The young woman had gotten her high school equivalency certificate; acquired subsidized work experience and vocational skills; improved her decisionmaking, problem-solving, and other life management skills; and arranged child care. She was ready to take the big step toward employment and self-sufficiency.

But the economics did not work. The jobs she had been offered—with low wages, limited hours, and no health benefits—would make her less well off than she would be if she stayed home and continued to receive AFDC and related benefits, especially when work expenses were factored in. The irony for the director was that she knew the program had succeeded when the participant had been able to calculate the complicated benefit–cost equation for work versus welfare and had felt a responsibility to ask how she could put her family at risk by going to work.

MDRC's studies of state welfare-to-work programs have shown that many women leave welfare for low-paying jobs, and in so doing trade "leisure" for no noticeable gain in income. Economics obviously is only one factor in the equation; the stigma of welfare and the broader promises of a job are other strong forces, and people respond. But clearly the deck is often stacked against work, and in pushing poor people to work, we are often asking them to make the very choices that I was taught in graduate school a rational person should reject.

Potential Policies to Make Work Pay

What actions can the federal and the state governments take to alter the equation and encourage welfare recipients to work? And how do these approaches affect attainment of the other societal goal: providing a decent standard of living for America's children at an affordable cost?

One strategy to make work pay is to make welfare less attractive by reducing real benefits and deepening the stigma of being on the dole. This is the strategy that most states have followed by default over the last twenty years, as AFDC benefits have lagged inflation and thus have been eroded 42 percent in real terms; and it is a strategy that some states are now proposing more consciously, in reaction to the recent rise in caseloads and a perceived crisis in welfare spending. Some proposals go beyond benefit cuts to limit the amount of time someone can receive welfare benefits. Clearly, cutting grants further will save money and increase work incentives, but the effect on the welfare rolls is less certain, and obviously this approach will do little to reduce the poverty gap.

A second approach to making work more profitable is for policymakers and administrators to reduce the cuts in welfare grants people sustain when they go to work, or to augment wages or provide complementary income to working families through actions outside the welfare system. These actions include adopting a child support assurance system, instituting a refundable tax credit for families with children, increasing the earned income tax credit (EITC), expanding health insurance and child care subsidies to the working poor, increasing the minimum wage, and providing guaranteed jobs for welfare recipients who cannot find unsubsidized work. Advocates of these "nonwelfare" reforms argue that poor women will not be able to work their way out of poverty, even after participating in education and training programs; that reducing child poverty should have priority; and that the country should substitute for categorical policies programs that reward equally the working and the welfare poor. If generous, this approach is likely to be substantially more expensive, with unknown effects on work effort, but it is more certain to reduce child poverty.

A third strategy is to redefine the social contract expressed in the AFDC program. This strategy calls for a shift from viewing AFDC as an income-conditioned entitlement to construing it as a set of reciprocal obligations whose goal is self-sufficiency for welfare recipients. This approach requires recipients to look for and accept a job, participate in some form of employment-directed activities, or risk losing some welfare benefits. At the same time, it requires government to provide not only a cash grant but also services designed to help the recipient obtain employment. This reformulation of AFDC began with the Work Incentive (WIN) program and was expanded and reaffirmed in the Job Opportunities and Basic Skills Training (JOBS) provisions of the Family Support Act of 1988. In its 1980s version (low- to moderate-cost services stressing immediate job placement), this approach saved money and increased work but did little to reduce poverty. The 1990s version emphasizes basic skills education and other intensive services, covering women with preschool children, requiring schooling for young mothers, and targeting groups at high risk of long-term welfare receipt—notably, teen-age mothers who have dropped out of school. How successful this latest version will be in getting people better jobs through education and training is not yet known.

For the past twenty years, state and federal policymakers have used all three of these approaches to encourage work: AFDC grants have been cut, payments to the working poor have expanded, and states have more or less mandated participation in activities focused on immediate employment. The combined result is that in 1991 real AFDC outlays were roughly the same as they were in 1971 and rates of child poverty were higher. Reality is thus at odds with the prevailing view of an AFDC program in crisis; at least, the crisis confronts children receiving AFDC, not taxpayers. The strategies of the 1980s have succeeded in discouraging welfare—leaving aside the current recession, caseloads have not grown so fast as the demographics would suggest—but they have failed to provide security for children.

WIN and JOBS: What Do We Know?

Although all three approaches may encourage work, no direct evidence bears on the effectiveness of making welfare less attractive or making work more attractive. For the welfare-to-work strategy, however, we have reliable data on what can and cannot be achieved.

WIN and JOBS, it should first be noted, mean very different things to different people. Such differences reflect divergent views about basic goals and thus the appropriate tools of reform. Some state and local administrators emphasize raising earnings and reducing poverty; others, cutting welfare costs. These different emphases translate into program designs that assign different priorities to the obligations of welfare recipients and government. Some administrators give priority to the improvement of job skills so that welfare recipients can get employment that will assure them a decent standard of living; others focus on enforcing participation in the program and maximizing immediate job placements.

JOBS has more federal matching funds than WIN and requires that states serve all adult recipients with children three years of age or older. Yet no state has—or will have—the resources to provide comprehensive services to everyone in this group. It is doubtful that resources will enable most states to provide even low-cost services for the full mandated caseload. Thus, in striving to meet their goals, administrators have to choose among three strategies. They can operate a program of low-cost services (primarily job search assistance) for a large share of the caseload; they can provide more expensive, higher-cost education and training services and case management to a more narrowly defined group; or they can mix low- and higher-cost services and reach a share of the caseload somewhere between those the other two options reach.

During the 1980s, under the WIN and WIN demonstration programs, most states followed the first strategy and provided low-cost job search and work experience. The JOBS legislation inclines states toward the mixed strategy through its dual emphasis on serving more people and providing some intensive services.

JOBS is too new to have produced data on its results, and studies of programs that have most of the features of JOBS have yet to be completed. Fortunately, studies were made in the 1980s of mixed strategies and of a few demonstrations that tested more intensive programs. They examined not only small-scale demonstration programs but also full-scale programs implemented by regular staff within ongoing welfare systems. These programs were operating in diverse environments and under both strong and weak economic conditions. They involved 65,000 people in twenty-one states.

Overwhelming evidence from these studies shows that work programs for single mothers on AFDC can be successful. Unequivocally, the studies show that different types of welfare-to-work programs produced sustained increases in employment and reductions in welfare receipt. Some programs were also highly cost effective: The investment yielded a clear and rapid payoff, returned to taxpayers as much as $3 per $1 invested, and reduced welfare costs for the WIN-mandated group as much as 19 percent.[1]

Using adjectives to characterize program effects can be dangerous, and over the years I have usually called these results "modest." My aim was to temper grandiose claims with realism and to caution that this approach appeared to offer no panacea. But some have taken "modest" to mean "trivial"—clearly not the case here. Some of the largest and most consistent effects to date have come from the mixed-strategy program in San Diego, the Saturation Work Initiative Model (SWIM), which enforced

---

1. Gueron and Pauly (1991). The picture for men, which is based on less evidence, is less positive. One reason is that the men who enrolled in these programs did much better on their own (as shown by the behavior of a control group) than did the women; thus, welfare-to-work programs for men had a harder time beating the control group. The women, in contrast, did relatively poorly on their own, and the programs proved to have a significant impact.

a requirement that participants undertake a fixed sequence of activities, starting with job search and work experience and continuing with education and training for those who did not thereafter get a job. For single mothers who were already on welfare (a more disadvantaged group than new applicants), SWIM increased average earnings $889 (or 50 percent) and reduced average AFDC payments $608 (or 13 percent) in the second year of follow-up.[2] It also had a major effect on work. For the same group, employment rates increased 10 percentage points: Approximately 50 percent of the single mothers required to participate in SWIM worked during a year, compared with 40 percent of those who were not required to participate.[3] I know of no reliable evidence that any other approach to welfare reform has resulted in a comparable increase in employment, let alone one that has done so while saving taxpayers money.

These findings on welfare-to-work programs are particularly striking in the current environment, in which people are searching for ideas to reduce welfare by modifying personal behavior. All of the evidence suggests that modifying behavior will be extremely difficult, yet, according to the studies, the approach relying on participation and work requirements can work. If policymakers seek to reduce the welfare rolls and increase employment, one task is clear: to put in place in the JOBS program across the country the best practices of state welfare-to-work programs identified by these studies.

These strong and consistent findings are especially important because they counter the apparently unshakable skepticism about the efficacy of government and because, under the current pressure on state budgets, a substantial share of the federal funds for state JOBS programs remains unspent.[4]

Other critical findings illuminate the tradeoffs implicit in program designs and the limitations of using the WIN or JOBS approach alone. In essence, the studies—again, of programs that offered little education and training—point to five basic conclusions:[5]

- If the goal is maximizing welfare savings, programs that begin by having people look for jobs do best.
- If the goal is getting people better jobs, more intensive strategies seem to do best, though the evidence is limited.

---

2. Because these averages include everyone who was required to be in the program—many of whom did not participate, receive any services, or obtain a job—they mask the much higher gains of those who took part in the program.

3. Hamilton and Friedlander (1989).

4. Congressional Budget Office staff report that, in fiscal year 1991, states drew down only 59 percent of federal matching funds for JOBS.

5. Gueron and Pauly (1991); Friedlander and Gueron (1992).

- If the goal is reaching the most disadvantaged, there is no clear guidance on what to do, but clearly job search activities alone are not adequate to increase employment and earnings.
- If the goals are multiple, a mixed strategy of low-cost services for some and carefully targeted higher-cost services for others is suggested.
- If the goal is substantially increasing the rate at which families and children move out of poverty, none of the pre-JOBS programs studied to date seems to have worked.

This last point is crucial. The findings suggest that most people who went to work as a result of welfare-to-work programs obtained relatively low-paying jobs. The ensuing reductions in their welfare grants often substantially offset earnings gains so that their incomes increased very little.

The results to date are relatively plain. The controversy is around their implications for policy, since they suggest that conclusions will differ depending on the weight given to particular goals. In other words, what you are after will shape your preference about program design, a circumstance suggesting the need for administrators to clarify their goals and make choices. The 1980s programs that mandated job search and immediate job placement plainly can encourage employment and save welfare funds. On this point, we have the strongest evidence. But if the goal is increasing the self-sufficiency of long-term recipients— as stated in the JOBS legislation—or increasing skills in order to get people into better jobs that may move families out of poverty, the evidence shows that job search alone will be inadequate. These limitations provide the rationale for the emphasis JOBS puts on education and training. The hope is that these more intensive services and targeting by JOBS on potential long-term recipients will succeed with the more disadvantaged, get people markedly better jobs, and result in more substantial increases in family income. If it does these things, JOBS may avoid the tradeoff suggested by the achievements and limitations of the earlier programs.

Although some of the previous studies of mixed-strategy programs offer hope, the current JOBS evaluation, sponsored by the U.S. Department of Health and Human Services, must answer whether the new program delivers on this promise and more effectively meets the two goals of our welfare system: encouraging work and reducing child poverty.

Improved Work Incentives
and Nonwelfare Income

In recent years, JOBS-like programs have carried much of the burden of encouraging families to work. The new emphasis on education and training may increase the average effects; but the limited earnings capacity of most women on welfare, combined with stagnating or falling wages for the low-skilled, constrains success. Even if they work full-time, the majority of women receiving AFDC are not likely to earn much more than they receive on welfare, particularly in high-grant states.[6]

The provisions of the Family Support Act for transitional child care and Medicaid and the recent increase in the EITC are significant. Even with these changes, however, many mothers on welfare face the dilemma of the New Chance participant I described earlier and have little economic incentive to choose work over welfare. That they continue to make that choice in fairly large numbers in the face of the short-term economic calculus that argues against it is a striking statement about the human spirit and about how much people want to get off welfare. This is where nonwelfare reforms designed to make work pay come in. Reforms outside the welfare system may make reform within it more effective by creating incentives that buttress, rather than undermine, our strongest values.

If the goal is increasing self-sufficiency, we must assure that JOBS is fully implemented and continue to make other changes that tilt the economic balance in favor of work.

While the Congress debates which changes to make, state administrators have been struggling to address the dilemma of the New Chance participant, a dilemma they hear about constantly from their staffs. Ten states have already acted to reduce the rate at which welfare grants are cut for people who go to work. Others are proposing more far-reaching changes in work incentives, including in one case the implementation of David Ellwood's proposal to limit the time welfare is paid and to provide community services jobs at the end. The most striking proposal is the subject of a demonstration we are working on with the Canadian government. Under that system, for the first time, benefits would be conditioned on full-time employment; for those long-term welfare recipients willing to work full-time, income would go up substantially.

In the past fifteen years, we have been learning about the potential that welfare-to-work strategies have to encourage work. Studies now

---

6. Sawhill (1976), pp. 201–11; Garfinkel and McLanahan (1986); Gueron (1990), pp. 79–98.

in place should largely complete the picture. But we know little about the costs and effects of the other strategies under discussion today. One challenge over the next five years will be to understand whether, and if so at what cost, those policies can deliver on their promise to reach the dual objectives of self-sufficiency and child welfare within a system better attuned to our society's values.

References

Friedlander, Daniel, and Judith M. Gueron. "Are High-Cost Services More Effective Than Low-Cost Services? Evidence From Experimental Evaluations of Welfare-to-Work Programs," in Charles Manski and Irwin Garfinkel, eds., *Evaluating Welfare and Training Programs*. Cambridge: Harvard University Press, 1992.

Garfinkel, Irwin, and Sara S. McLanahan. *Single Mothers and Their Children: A New American Dilemma*. Washington: The Urban Institute Press, 1986.

Gueron, Judith M. "Work and Welfare: Lessons on Employment Programs," *Journal of Economic Perspectives*, vol. 4 (Winter 1990), pp. 79–98.

_____, and Edward Pauly. *From Welfare to Work*. New York: Russell Sage Foundation, 1991.

Hamilton, Gayle, and Daniel Friedlander. *Final Report on the Saturation Work Initiative Model in San Diego*. New York: Manpower Demonstration Research Corporation, 1989.

Sawhill, Isabel, "Discrimination and Poverty among Women Who Head Families," *Signs*, vol. 1 (Autumn 1976), pp. 201–11.

WORK AND POVERTY: WHAT IS THE PROBLEM?

Lawrence M. Mead

T he main reason work does not pay for today's poor is that most of them do not do enough of it. The reasons are unclear. The government can do certain things to make work pay better, but above all it must do something to cause poor adults to put in steadier working hours. Without that, nothing done to increase the rewards of work will make much difference. Politically as well, the public will not support further moves to help the working-aged poor unless they work more.[1]

The Employment Problem

Overwhelmingly, families with children are needy today because the adults in these families do not work normal hours. Work levels among the poor have fallen over the last thirty years and are now considerably below those for the population as a whole. For the moment, I say nothing about causes. Table 1 shows the trends in employment for the heads of poor families from 1959 to 1990. The share of all heads of poor families with any earnings at all fell from 80 percent to 56 percent in

---

Lawrence M. Mead is an associate professor of politics at New York University.

1. Much of what follows is derived from Mead (1992), although that work does not focus specifically on families with children.

Table 1
Work Experience of Heads of Poor Families
with Children under 18,
Selected Years, 1959–90[1]
Percent

Type of family head and working status	1959	1970	1975	1985	1990
All poor heads					
Worked at any time	80	67	55	54	56
Worked full year and full time	41	28	17	17	17
Did not work	17	32	45	45	44
Poor female heads					
Worked at any time	43	46	38	40	45
Worked full year and full time	9	7	6	7	8
Did not work	57	54	62	60	55
Other poor heads					
Worked at any time	90	84	75	72	74
Worked full year and full time	50	45	29	30	31
Did not work	6	14	24	26	26

Sources: U.S. Department of Commerce, Bureau of the Census, Series P-60, no. 68, table 10 (for 1959); no. 81, table 23 (1970); no. 106, table 27 (1975); no. 158, table 21 (1985); and no. 175, table 19 (1990).

1. Full year means at least 50 weeks a year; full time means at least 35 hours a week. Other heads means male heads in 1959–75, heads other than single mothers in 1985, and husbands of married-couple families in 1990. Components may not sum to totals because of rounding or the omission of workers in the armed forces.

that period, and the share working the full year and full time fell even more sharply, from 41 to 17 percent. The last five years may have seen an upturn in work effort, but statistically no clear change has occurred since 1978; most of the decline took place earlier.[2]

Much of the decline in work reflects the growing gap between the poverty level and average earnings since 1959. As real wages rose, most of the working poor earned their way out of poverty. It is now difficult to work normal hours and remain poor, so almost by definition few of the remaining poor are employed steadily. If poverty were

2. U.S. Department of Commerce (1991), p. 8.

defined relative to average incomes, rather than in the absolute terms of the official measure, poverty and employment would not diverge so clearly. Even if we define poverty as the bottom fifth of the income distribution, however, a fall in work levels among families with children is still apparent.[3]

The decline in work is not due to a fall in the share of the poor who are of working age, that is, those other than children or the elderly. That share has actually risen since 1959, and is now just under a half of all the poor. Rather, the decline is linked to the growth in the number of families with female heads at the bottom of society. The fall results because there are more such families, not because poor female heads are themselves working less; as the table shows, their work level has always been low. However, the decline in work is not an automatic result of this growth. Among the black poor, who account for most of the long-term poor, two-thirds of poor families headed by females were needy before the breakup of the parents as well as after, equally because of nonwork.[4] As the table shows, even among heads other than single mothers, most of whom are husbands in two-parent families, work has declined markedly. Even if one excludes from the employable those who are elderly, disabled, or students, or who have children under age six, the share of poor family heads who could work has risen, and the share actually working has fallen.[5]

This fall in employment among the poor has occurred at a time when work levels for the general population have reached new heights. Because women and members of the baby-boom generation have been flooding to work, and because families are struggling to keep up with inflation on stagnant wages, about two-thirds of American adults are working or seeking work today, the highest proportion in history. For families with children, average working hours have jumped for both intact and female-headed families, especially among the affluent.[6] Among family heads, the change is less dramatic, as most of them were already employed. Table 2 shows the trends in employment among all heads of families with children. There has been a slight fall in employment overall, reflecting the decline at the bottom of society, but a considerable rise for female heads. Since the latter include nonworking welfare mothers, the rise for female heads not receiving welfare is even more dramatic.

Table 3 compares work levels among the general population and the poor for individuals and for several groupings of family heads in 1990. In all categories, the difference is enormous. The proportion of

3. U.S. Congressional Budget Office (1988), table A–15.
4. Bane (1986), pp. 22–31.
5. Danziger and Gottschalk (1986), pp. 17–18.
6. Congressional Budget Office (1988), table A–15.

Table 2
Work Experience of Heads of All Families with Children under 18,
Selected Years, 1970–90[1]
Percent

Type of family head and working status	1970	1975	1985	1990
All heads				
Worked at any time	91	88	86	89
Worked full year and full time	71	67	66	67
Did not work	7	10	12	11
Female heads				
Worked at any time	61	63	66	69
Worked full year and full time	26	31	38	40
Did not work	39	37	34	31
Other heads				
Worked at any time	95	93	91	95
Worked full year and full time	77	73	73	76
Did not work	2	5	6	5

Sources: U.S. Department of Commerce, Bureau of the Census, Series P-60, no. 81, table 23 (for 1970); no. 106, table 27 (1975); no. 158, table 21 (1985); and no. 175, table 19 (1990).

1. Full year means at least 50 weeks a year; full time means at least 35 hours a week. Other heads means male heads in 1959–75, heads other than single mothers in 1985, and husbands of married-couple families in 1990. Components may not sum to totals because of rounding or the omission of workers in the armed forces.

those working is half to three-quarters higher for the general population than for the poor; for full year, full time work, the proportion is four or five times higher. The contrast would be still greater if one contrasted the poor with the nonpoor rather than with the whole population.

These differences account directly for most of today's family poverty. Table 4 shows how poverty rates vary with work levels for the same demographic groups, and reveals the potent effects of employment on poverty. A nonworker is from two and three-quarters to six times as likely to be poor as is a worker. Eighty percent of female heads are poor if they do not work; only 9 percent—under the average for the population—are poor if they work the full year and full time. Of course, the contrasts would not be so great if one allowed for other factors that affect

Table 3
Employment Status of Persons 16 and over and of Family Heads,
by Income Level, 1990[1]
Percent

Income level and working status	Persons	All heads	With children under 18 All heads	With children under 18 Female heads
All income levels				
Worked at any time	70	78	89	69
Worked full year and full time	42	58	67	40
Did not work	30	22	11	31
Income below poverty				
Worked at any time	41	51	56	45
Worked full year and full time	10	15	17	8
Did not work	59	49	44	55

Sources: U.S. Department of Commerce, Bureau of the Census, *Poverty in the United States: 1990*, Series P-60, no. 175, tables 14 and 19.
1. Full year means at least 50 weeks a year; full time means at least 35 hours a week.

Table 4
Poverty Rates of Persons 16 and over and of Family Heads
by Employment Status, 1990[1]
Percent

Working status	All persons	All heads	With children under 18 All heads	With children under 18 Female heads
Worked at any time	6.5	7.1	10.5	29.0
Worked full year and full time	2.5	2.9	4.1	9.1
Did not work	27.1	23.9	66.1	79.7
Total	11.2	10.8	16.6	44.5

Sources: U.S. Department of Commerce, Bureau of the Census, *Poverty in the United States: 1990*, Series P-60, no. 175, tables 14 and 19.
1. Full year means at least 50 weeks a year; full time means at least 35 hours a week.

poverty, such as wage differences. No single variable can compete with employment, however, in determining whether families are poor.

Nonwork would be a problem for poor families quite aside from the consequences for income. It contributes to the problems of lifestyle that, as much as low income, conspire to keep people needy today. One reason why needy children typically do poorly in school and then on the job is that they do not observe their parents functioning consistently in the world of work.

Do Low Wages and Benefits Cause Poverty?

These figures strongly suggest that the main economic problem for poor families is sheer lack of employment, not the failure of work to pay enough. If half of all poor family heads, and three-fifths of all poor adults, do not work at all, then whether wages or benefits could be higher has little to do with their predicament. Although a thin majority of poor family heads with children have some earnings in a year, non-workers vastly outnumber full time workers—2.5 million to 0.9 million in 1990.[7]

Arguments that the main cause of family poverty is low wages are unpersuasive. It is not true, for example, that the culprit is the minimum wage. In 1985, only 19 percent of minimum-wage workers were poor, while only 26 percent of poor workers earned at or below the minimum wage. Escaping poverty, then, depends more on hours worked than on wage levels. Moreover, whether or not one lives in poverty depends on the overall income of a family, not on one worker's earnings. One person working at the minimum wage, even the full year and full time, cannot support a whole family, of course, but very few family heads are in this position. Most earn above the minimum or can count on other workers in the family. In 1985, only 710,000 workers at the minimum wage or below were the sole worker in a poor family, and only 120,000 were working full time year-round in a poor family.[8] The recent increase in the minimum wage has no doubt reduced the link between the minimum and poverty still further.

Family poverty also has little connection to low wages in general. As table 4 suggests, very few steady workers are poor. Even low-wage workers today are seldom poor, and even more seldom are they the heads of poor families. Between 1959 and 1984, the share of workers earning less than half the average private-sector wage who were poor fell from 42 percent to 18 percent, and the share of such workers

---

7. U.S. Department of Commerce (1991), table 19.
8. U.S. Congressional Budget Office (1986), pp. 15–16, 18–19.

heading poor families fell from 24 percent to 7 percent. By 1984, the remaining poor, low-wage family heads numbered only 1 million, or 1 percent of all wage and salary workers. They remained poor mainly because they worked fewer hours than the nonpoor and because fewer members of their families worked.[9]

Low wages are perhaps most critical for single mothers, who must attempt to support families alongside child care responsibilities, and often on one income. Whether such mothers escape poverty obviously depends on child support and the cost of child care as well as wages. However, the best estimate is that at least half of dependent mothers could escape welfare if they worked full time.[10] The great majority of single mothers who avoid welfare and poverty do work full time.[11] As table 2 shows, that is the norm for family heads with children. Society may decide it does not want single mothers to have to work this hard. Nevertheless, the initial cause of poverty remains low working hours rather than low wages.

To contend that low returns to work are central to poverty, one would have to show that low wages or benefits are a cause, not only of working poverty, but of nonwork. Perhaps low returns discourage people from working, and higher wages or benefits would draw more poor adults into the labor force. The gain in income from raising work levels would then dwarf the gain due to higher wages by themselves. However, there is no evidence that the work effort of poor people responds much to higher wages. Employment of welfare mothers is not much affected by the level of welfare benefits, nor by the wages the mothers are able to earn.[12]

A related theory has been that recipients are deterred from working by fear of losing health coverage. They get Medicaid while on welfare, but many low-wage jobs lack health insurance. In fact, this effect seems to be confined to the families with the worst health problems. It does not account for the extent of nonwork now found among the dependent.[13]

None of the above implies that low wages or benefits are unimportant. Perhaps unskilled workers are unrewarded. Certainly, the minimum wage is below historic levels relative to average wages, and many workers lack health coverage. But these are problems for workers much more than for the nonworking poor. They help to explain *inequality among people who are employed*. They do not, on the whole, explain *failure*

---

9. Burkhauser and Finegan (1989), pp. 59–60.
10. Michalopoulos and Garfinkel (1989).
11. U.S. Congress (1990), p. 1029.
12. Moffitt (1983), p. 1033, and (1986), pp. 389–439.
13. Blank (1989), and Moffitt and Wolfe (1990).

to work at all, which is the main economic problem among the poor, especially the long-term cases.

Would Higher Wages and Benefits Help?

Just as low wages and benefits do not seem to be a major cause of poverty, so increasing the returns to work would only marginally ease the plight of poor families. It would make them only slightly better off in a material sense, and it might exacerbate the employment problem.

The Congress raised the minimum wage to $4.35 an hour in 1989. It might raise it again. The trouble is that most of the benefit would go to the better-off, simply because most minimum wage workers are already above poverty. Because relatively few poor people work at or near the minimum, raising the floor is no longer an effective antipoverty strategy.[14] One could also increase the earned income tax credit (EITC). In 1990, Congress raised the EITC to about 17 percent of the first $7,140 of earned income in 1991, and added an adjustment for family size. Since EITC targets the subsidy directly on poor workers, increasing it would be the most efficient way to help the working poor.

Neither measure is likely to reduce family poverty very much, however, because neither has shown a power to raise working hours. In fact, increases may depress hours. A higher minimum wage probably reduces work levels because it eliminates some jobs, and leads some youths to withdraw from the labor force. A higher minimum wage and a higher EITC also reduce work effort, because low-wage workers who benefit can earn the same income with fewer working hours. This motivation is apparently stronger than the incentive to work more hours that is generated by raising the returns per hour. In the terms economists use, the income effect dominates the substitution effect. Although these reductions are probably small, they exacerbate the political problem caused by nonwork.[15]

Another approach to increasing payoffs is to try to weaken the disincentives in welfare that many believe deter the dependent from working. Liberals try to do this by strengthening work incentives, that is, by reducing the proportion of earned income that welfare recipients must return to the government in the form of reduced assistance. Conservatives prefer to do it simply by reducing the number of employed or employable people who can get on welfare at all. The trouble is that neither strategy has much affected work levels. The work incentives that operated in AFDC between 1967 and 1981 did not

---

14. Burkhauser and Finegan (1989), pp. 53, 61–64.
15. Brown and others (1982), pp. 497–99, and Burtless (1989), pp. 136–37.

palpably raise work effort among recipients, and the Reagan cuts in those incentives in 1981 did not lower it. Moreover, incentives may reduce work levels among low-income workers not currently on welfare, as they can now more easily qualify for assistance.[16] These disappointments caused most experts and politicians to turn away from changing work incentives as a means of reforming welfare.

Besides a higher EITC, the most useful work-connected benefit would probably be guaranteed health care. Most poor children, however, are already covered by recent extensions of Medicaid, whether or not their parents are on welfare. Much of what looks like inadequate care may really reflect the failure of poor parents to exploit fully the programs and benefits already available. And, in any event, expanded health care would do little to augment the cash flow of the poor. Here, again, solutions depend mainly on raising working hours.

The great limitation of strategies to make work pay through increasing benefits is that they assume more work rather than motivating it. Additional benefits would be of real value *if* the poor worked enough to gain from them. But if they worked enough, they would be unlikely to be poor for long anyway. Because most poor adults do not work steadily, increasing the benefits from work would not help them much. Higher work-related benefits tend to reach only the transiently poor, the families that already have working members and are, for that reason, likely to be needy only a year or two. They do not reach the chronic cases, especially those that arouse the most concern—long-term welfare recipients and their children, who often stay out of the labor market for years at a stretch.

It is important that work pay enough. As David Ellwood says, "If you work, you shouldn't be poor." Unfortunately, satisfying that "if" is most of the difficulty. Work-connected benefits address an important problem, but, on the whole, a different one from poverty. They are a way to make workers more equal in their rewards, a traditional goal of American social policy. They do little, however, to make more poor adults into workers, which is much the more important challenge today.

The Political Problem

Of course, our society could simply decide to give poor families whatever they need to escape poverty and attenuate any connection to work. We could raise work-connected benefits to a much higher level, so that anyone with earnings would thereby qualify for a living income. In

---

16. Levy (1979).

the extreme case, we could guarantee anyone who worked at all in a year a poverty-level income, with associated health care and other benefits.

We could also dispense with any work connection and cure poverty with straight income transfers. One form of this idea now in vogue is more generous child support. Simply tightening up the enforcement of child support on absent parents, however, may make little dent in poverty or in the welfare rolls. In the case of most welfare families, the absent fathers simply do not make enough to lift their dependents off the rolls; they are often jobless themselves. Until collections improve, child support could reduce poverty substantially only if families received an assured benefit whether or not the fathers paid support. A more straightforward transfer would be some form of family allowance, for example, the guaranteed income plans of the 1960s and 1970s, or the $1,000 refundable tax credit for families with children recently recommended by the National Commission on Children.

Strong economic objections can be raised to all these devices: They impose work disincentives and costs. Although one might want to confine the new benefits to the current poor, they would in all equity have to be extended to all low-income workers, and thus would levy a tremendous burden on the economy.

The fundamental problem, however, is political. Since the early 1970s, the public has made clear, through its elected representatives, that it will not tolerate further transfers to the working-aged poor unless something is done to cure the perceived abuses in welfare, particularly nonwork by employable adults. Failure to take the work issue seriously was the main reason why the Nixon and Carter welfare reform plans were defeated in the Congress.[17]

For the same reason, as well as because of fears about costs, the recent transfer proposals are unlikely to receive serious consideration. Assured child support, it is claimed, would generate a strong work incentive, since earnings would not reduce the benefit. But like other incentives, this would induce welfare recipients to raise working hours only slightly, and it might induce other workers to work less.[18] The National Commission on Children treated work as a *problem* government should solve, not, as the public thinks of it, as an *obligation* the recipients owe.[19]

"Making work pay" is an attractive strategy precisely because it satisfies the work ethic. Benefits go only to employees and their families. The difficulty is that such programs cannot reach the seriously poor, who are the least likely to work. On the other hand, welfare, which does

---

17. Mead (1986), chap. 5.
18. Garfinkel and others (1990), pp. 16–18.
19. National Commission on Children (1991), pp. 104–09.

reach them, lacks a work condition and is thus unpopular and under-funded. Social policy cannot escape that dilemma as long as most of the poor continue not to work.

Much of the recent thinking in income maintenance amounts to an effort to square that circle. One tactic is to build a greater welfare element into existing subsidies. This is what a higher EITC, the family adjustment for EITC, and the assured child-support benefit do. The theory is that somebody is earning these benefits, either the recipient or the absent father. But the subsidies are less closely tied to employment than is the original EITC or child-support collections, and the danger is that they would be seen as no different from current welfare programs.

The other tactic is to create some new entitlement that serves everyone, thus submerging the poor in a much larger, and generally working, population. That is the rationale of assured child support, which in theory serves all single mothers, and the proposed child tax credit. Allegedly, the assured child-support benefit is like social insurance because it is not just for the poor. Unfortunately, no legerdemain can convince the public that such benefits are distinct from welfare, whose hallmark has become that its recipients do not work. The assured benefit and the child tax credit are, in fact, unlike social insurance because they are not contributory and because the recipients cannot claim to have "earned" them.

What makes a program respectable is not its formal structure but whether the recipients are considered respectable. The problem for the poor is that they do not behave in "respectable" ways—especially, they do not work—not that they receive mean-tested benefits. In Europe, poverty and middle-class programs are less distinct than they are in the United States, but transfers to people of working age have become almost as unpopular as they are here, and for the same reason—because of the recipients' failure to work and other perceived "abuses" of benefits. By the same token, a means test is not a bar to popularity if the program requires work—witness the vogue for the EITC in the Congress.

Raising Work Levels

My conclusion is that raising work levels among poor adults is indispensable to alleviating family poverty. Work-connected benefits cannot do the whole job, or even most of it. How could work levels be raised? The answer requires finding the cause of the failure to work, but the cause is not at all clear. Typically, analysts have sought to identify some barrier that keeps most poor parents from working steadily. While low wages and low benefits are two prime candidates, others are a total lack of jobs, racial bias, welfare disincentives, and a lack of elemental skills or child care.

My own reading of the evidence suggests that, though each of these may explain a small part of the work problem, none—either individually or collectively—can account for the current extent of nonwork among the poor. As one proof of this reading, no benefit designed to remove barriers—work incentives, voluntary training programs, child care programs—has had any palpable effect on work levels. My conclusion is that the main cause of nonwork lies elsewhere, probably in the heritage of the heavily poor ethnic groups and in weaknesses of public authority. Most of the long-term poor are black, Hispanic, and Native American. The main reasons they do not work at higher levels seem to be that, in view of the history of their groups, they believe opportunities are not available to them. Also, welfare and other social programs seldom require them to work, so they do not discover the opportunities that steady work would bring.[20]

The drift of federal social policy has been toward requiring work by the dependent. This approach shows more potential than any other. Recent work programs linked to welfare have substantially increased the employment and earnings of clients. More important, in my view, they raise the work effort of clients quite sharply. Recipients involved in the recent programs participate in employment, job search, or training at twice the rate, at least, of recipients not subject to them. "Workfare" defined in this broad sense—not simply as unpaid work in government jobs—is the most promising strategy to emerge in welfare. That explains why the main purpose of the Family Support Act of 1988 (FSA), the most recent welfare reform, is to expand work programs.

My recommendation is simply to implement the Family Support Act fully. Some states are having difficulty satisfying the participation targets set in the act, which requires that at least 20 percent of employable recipients participate in workfare by 1995. It is vital that the participation targets be met. The higher the proportion of the employable clients that participate actively, the greater will be the gains from workfare. In my view, high participation can be achieved only if the programs are mandatory, although FSA does not directly impose this requirement. The more dependent welfare recipients will not work unless they are required to work as a condition of support.[21]

I realize that it remains controversial to require the poor to work. Most analysts prefer that work programs be voluntary, not mandatory. But what is the goal? Is it to liberate the poor, to remove the pressures that burden their lives? Or is it to deal with their income problems in a

---

20. Mead (1992), chaps. 4–7.
21. Mead (1988), (1990).

way that integrates them more fully into American life? If the former, then income transfers are the best option in theory, but in practice they have little chance before the Congress or the public. If the latter, then work levels must be raised, and doing so will take mandatory work standards. Under current conditions, one cannot both take pressure off the poor in the short run and help them improve their lot substantially in the long run. A serious work policy must place real demands on the poor, but it would gain them higher earnings and much greater public support.

By tradition, helping the poor and requiring them to help themselves are seen as opposites. To demand that the poor work more is tantamount to saying government should do less for them. I think this perspective is pernicious. Self-help and government help are not opposed; quite the contrary. In America, the two go together. Those who work steadily also get the most aid from government, and those who do not get very little. The middle class benefits from the mainstream income and health programs, which are much more generous than welfare; it justifies these on grounds that it has earned them through work. The poor get only the scraps from the government's table, primarily because most of them do not work regularly. If they worked more, poor families would get much more from *both* the private and the public sector than they do now.

References

Bane, Mary Jo. "Household Composition and Poverty," in Sheldon H. Danziger and Daniel H. Weinberg, eds., *Fighting Poverty: What Works and What Doesn't*. Cambridge: Harvard University Press, 1986.

Blank, Rebecca M. "The Effect of Medical Need and Medicaid on AFDC Participation," *Journal of Human Resources*, vol. 24, no. 1 (1989), pp. 54–87.

Brown, Charles, and others. "The Effect of the Minimum Wage on Employment and Unemployment," *Journal of Economic Literature*, vol. 20, no. 2 (1982), pp. 487–528.

Burkhauser, Richard V., and T. Aldrich Finegan. "The Minimum Wage and the Poor: The End of a Relationship," *Journal of Policy Analysis and Management*, vol. 8, no. 1 (1989), pp. 53–71.

Burtless, Gary. "The Effect of Reform on Employment, Earnings, and Income," in Phoebe H. Cottingham and David T. Ellwood, eds., *Welfare Policy for the 1990s*. Cambridge: Harvard University Press, 1989.

Danziger, Sheldon, and Peter Gottschalk. "Work, Poverty, and the Working Poor: A Multifaceted Problem," *Monthly Labor Review*, vol. 109, no. 9 (1986), pp. 17–21.

Garfinkel, Irwin, and others. "The Wisconsin Child Support Assurance System: Estimated Effects on Poverty, Labor Supply, Caseloads, and Cost," *Journal of Human Resources*, vol. 25, no. 1 (1990), pp. 1–31.

Levy, Frank. "The Labor Supply of Female Household Heads, or AFDC Work Incentives Don't Work Too Well," *Journal of Human Resources*, vol. 14, no. 1 (1979), pp. 76–97.

Mead, Lawrence M. *The New Politics of Poverty: The Nonworking Poor in America*. New York: Basic Books, 1992.

_____. *Beyond Entitlement: The Social Obligations of Citizenship*. New York: Free Press, 1986.

_____. "Should Workfare Be Mandatory? What Research Says," *Journal of Policy Analysis and Management*, vol. 9, no. 3 (1990), pp. 400–04.

_____. "The Potential for Work Enforcement: A Study of WIN," *Journal of Policy Analysis and Management*, vol. 7, no. 2 (1988), pp. 264–88.

Michalopoulos, Charles, and Irwin Garfinkel. "Reducing the Welfare Dependence and Poverty of Single Mothers By Means of Earnings and Child Support: Wishful Thinking and Realistic Possibility." Madison: University of Wisconsin, Institute for Research on Poverty, 1989.

Moffitt, Robert. "Work Incentives in Transfer Programs (Revisited): A Study of the AFDC Program," in Ronald G. Ehrenberg, ed., *Research in Labor Economics*, vol. 8, part B (1986), pp. 389–439.

_____. "An Economic Model of Welfare Stigma," *American Economic Review*, vol. 73, no. 5 (1983), pp. 1023–35.

_____, and Barbara Wolfe. "The Effect of the Medicaid Program on Welfare Participation and Labor Supply." Madison: University of Wisconsin, Institute for Research on Poverty, 1990.

National Commission on Children. *Beyond Rhetoric: A New American Agenda for Children and Families*. Washington: Government Printing Office, 1991.

U.S. Congress, House of Representatives, Committee on Ways and Means, *Overview of Entitlement Programs: Background Materials and Data on Programs Within the Jurisdiction of the Committee on Ways and Means*. Washington: Government Printing Office, 1990.

U.S. Congressional Budget Office. *Trends in Family Income: 1970–1986*. Washington: Government Printing Office, 1988.

_____. "The Minimum Wage: Its Relationship to Incomes and Poverty." Staff Working Paper.Washington: CBO, 1986.

U.S. Department of Commerce, Bureau of the Census. *Poverty in the United States: 1990*. Series P-60, no. 175. Washington: Government Printing Office, 1991.

INCREASING THE
RETURNS TO WORK

Isaac Shapiro

Substantial work effort, including full-time year-round work, is common among poor families with children. In 1990, 66 percent of families with children in poverty had at least one worker. Seventeen percent included a full-time year-round worker. Because families with full-time year-round workers are slightly larger than other families, 25 percent of all people living in poor families with children live in families with a full-time year-round worker. About 5.5 million people live in such families.[1]

Moreover, the problems of the working poor have intensified. The past three or so decades can be broken into two periods. From 1959 to 1975, the proportion of the poor who were working declined. But the trend changed in 1975. From that year until 1990, the proportion of the poor who work has remained stable or has increased, depending upon which categories of poor are examined.

For example, among poor female heads of families, the proportion who worked increased from 38 percent in 1975 to 45 percent in 1990, as shown in table 1 of the paper by Lawrence M. Mead in this volume. Part of the increase reflects the fact that 1975 was a recession year with high unemployment. But even if comparable points in the economic cycle are examined, work effort among the poor increased.

Isaac Shapiro is a senior research analyst at the Center on Budget and Policy Priorities.

1. U.S. Bureau of the Census (1991).

In addition, the likelihood of working and remaining poor rose substantially over the 1980s. The proportion of the poor among working families with children rose more than one quarter, from 7.7 percent in 1979 to 9.7 percent in 1989 (both were peak years of economic recoveries).[2]

A study by Rebecca Blank of Northwestern University also suggests that the problem of the working poor has intensified. Blank compared the relative unresponsiveness of poverty to economic growth in the 1980s with the sharp fall in poverty during the period of economic growth in the 1960s. She found that work effort among the poor increased *more* during the recovery of the 1980s than during the recovery of the 1960s. The reason poverty didn't drop more in the 1980s is because wage rates fell.[3]

Policies affecting the working poor are important not only to the working poor themselves but also to nonworking poor families. People often change categories from year to year as they move in and out of the labor market; the jobs that become available to the nonworking poor are generally the same jobs that the working poor now hold.

The Minimum Wage

Two important changes in policy that would increase the returns to work are expanding the earned income tax credit and raising the minimum wage. I will skip over the consensus favorite, the earned income tax credit, and concentrate on the minimum wage.

The minimum wage remains below its historic level. It was not changed from 1981 to 1989 and thus fell in purchasing power. Less than half of the ground lost to inflation was recaptured when the minimum wage was then raised to its current level of $4.25 an hour. As a result, whereas in the 1960s and the 1970s, full-time work at the minimum wage typically lifted a family of three out of poverty, today full-time work at the minimum wage leaves that family about 20 percent below the poverty line.[4]

Even when earnings at the minimum wage are combined with the earned income tax credit, full-time work at the minimum wage leaves a family short of the poverty line. In 1992, the after-tax income of full-time minimum wage workers will fall $1,800 below the estimated

---

2. U.S. Bureau of the Census (1979), (1989).
3. Blank (1991).
4. Author's calculations.

poverty line for a family of three and $5,000 short of the estimated poverty line for a family of four.[5]

Although most minimum wage workers are not poor, the minimum wage is important to many of the working poor. Data from the Congressional Budget Office indicate that in 1987, 57 percent of poor workers had earnings at or near the minimum wage, earning $4.35 an hour or less.[6] It turns out that $4.35 an hour in 1987 matched the purchasing power of the minimum wage in the 1960s and 1970s, when full-time year-round work at the minimum wage lifted a family of three out of poverty. In 1992, the minimum wage would need to be $5.39 an hour to provide full-time earnings equal to the three-person poverty line.

The minimum wage has important practical advantages over some of the other proposals to make work pay, even some of those that are otherwise sound policies. For example, virtually all recipients of the earned income tax credit receive the credit in a lump sum at the end of the year when they file their tax return. The minimum wage, of course, comes with each paycheck.

Despite its advantages, some arguments have been raised against increasing the minimum wage. The most common is that it would price a large number of workers—particularly poor workers and low-skilled workers—out of the labor market. Several recent studies suggest that this argument is overstated.

One study, by Alison Wellington, used the time-series regression model developed in the 1960s and 1970s and perfected by Charles Brown and other economists at the Minimum Wage Study Commission.[7] Wellington updated and revised the commission's model using data through 1986; virtually all earlier studies relied on data from the 1960s and 1970s. Wellington found a smaller employment effect than the older studies did. Specifically, she found that a 10 percent increase in the minimum wage is associated with a 0.6 percent decrease in teenage employment: some effect, but a relatively modest one.

A second set of studies was conducted by David Card of Princeton University. One of his studies analyzed the labor market in California when the state raised its minimum wage above the federal level. This study compared employment trends in California and in other states, controlling for other factors. Card also studied the recent increase in the federal minimum wage and its effect on states with different proportions of low-wage workers. His findings are noteworthy. Not only did he find that increasing the minimum wage boosted incomes, he

---

5. Author's calculations. After-tax income equals earnings at the minimum wage plus the earned income tax credit minus the employee's share of payroll taxes.
6. U.S. Congressional Budget Office (1988).
7. Wellington (1991).

also found that it did not reduce employment. "Contrary to the implications of conventional economic models," he concluded, "I find no evidence that the rise in the minimum lowered teenage employment rates."[8]

A final set of studies was conducted by Lawrence Katz of Harvard University and Alan Krueger of Princeton University.[9] Katz and Krueger examined the effect of the recent increase in the minimum wage on the fast food industry in Texas. Their findings suggested that the employment effects of the recent minimum wage increase are, if anything, positive, not negative.

These studies do not prove that any increase in the minimum wage—no matter how large—would have only desirable effects. Instead, they suggest that the labor market is more complicated than is implied by the simple model, which holds that virtually any rise in the minimum wage results in a significant decrease in employment. Particularly when the minimum wage falls to low levels, raising it may have only a modest effect on employment. In setting the minimum wage, we must strike the right balance between increasing income and not significantly threatening employment.

Unemployment Insurance

Unemployment insurance (UI) should also be reformed to offer additional help to the working poor if they lose their jobs through no fault of their own.

The unemployment insurance system performed badly during most of the recent recession. From July 1990 to November 1991, only 40 percent of the unemployed received unemployment benefits in an average month; that is the lowest rate ever during a recession. Low-wage workers were especially unlikely to receive benefits.

In some months during the summer of 1991, more than 300,000 workers exhausted their state unemployment benefits but did not qualify for additional aid. This large number of exhaustees likely contributed to the sharp increase in the welfare rolls during this period.

In November 1991, the Congress and the President agreed on a temporary extension of unemployment insurance benefits, and that temporary extension was further strengthened in February 1992. What is needed, however, are permanent, comprehensive reforms to the unemployment insurance system. In many states the unemployed are unlikely to qualify even for the basic state benefits. In fourteen states fewer than one in three unemployed received benefits in 1991. Legislation enacted

---

8. Card (1991).
9. Katz and Krueger (March 1991), (November 1991).

in July 1992 improved assistance to the long-term unemployed but made virtually no improvement in the basic UI benefits on which jobless workers must rely during their first six months of unemployment.

Other Proposals

I will close with two other recommendations.

First, states also have a key role in establishing policies that would increase the returns to work. These state policies include not only child support assurance and welfare reform, which are discussed in other papers in this volume, but also earned income tax credits, which six states have already enacted, and reforms in unemployment insurance.

Second, work requirements must be coupled with public service jobs. Particularly in a recession, job opportunities are insufficient to enable all the nonworking poor to work—or to work more. But even as the economy recovers, not all of the poor will be able to find employment.

In sum, the problems of the working poor are significant and to some degree have grown during the 1980s. Fortunately, policies to assist the working poor are readily identifiable. It remains to be seen whether federal and state governments will choose to enact them.

References

Blank, Rebecca M. "Growth is Not Enough: Why the Recovery of the 1980s Did So Little to Reduce Poverty." Statement to the U.S. Congress, Joint Economic Committee, September 26, 1991.

Card, David. "Do Minimum Wages Reduce Employment? A Case Study of California, 1987–89." Working Paper No. 278. Princeton University, Industrial Relations Section, May 1991.

_____. "Using Regional Variation in Wages to Measure the Effects of the Federal Minimum Wage." Paper delivered at Cornell University Conference on New Minimum Wage Research, Ithaca, New York, November 15, 1991.

Katz, Lawrence, and Alan B Krueger. "The Effect of the New Minimum Wage Law in a Low-Wage Labor Market." Working Paper No. 3655. Cambridge: National Bureau of Economic Research, March 1991.

_____. "The Effect of the Minimum Wage on the Fast Food Industry." Paper delivered at Cornell University Conference on New Minimum Wage Research, Ithaca, New York, November 15, 1991.

Shapiro, Isaac, and Marion Nichols. *Far From Fixed: An Analysis of the Unemployment Insurance System.* Washington: Center on Budget and Policy Priorities, 1992.

U.S. Bureau of the Census. *Poverty in the United States.* Washington: Government Printing Office, 1979, 1989, and 1990.

U.S. Congressional Budget Office. Unpublished tabulations based on data from the Current Population Survey. Washington: CBO, March 1988.

Wellington, Alison J. "Effect of the Minimum Wage on the Employment Status of Youths: An Update," *Journal of Human Resources,* vol. 26 (Winter 1991), pp. 27–46.

WHAT COULD $10 BILLION OR $40 BILLION DO FOR CHILDREN?

Robert Greenstein

I have been asked two questions: If there were $40 billion a year in new funds for income security programs for children, how should we use it? Also, if $10 billion in new funds were available rather than $40 billion, how should that be used?

In thinking about these questions, I have had to establish two conventions. First, I must define income security. I have chosen to limit income security programs to those included in Function 600, Income Security, in the federal budget. Thus my proposals do not include areas such as health care, Head Start, education, or job training.

Second, I must decide how to treat those program expansions for which I have an accompanying financing proposal. If proposing a method to pay for an increase in spending meant that the spending would not count against the $40 billion or the $10 billion ceiling, the exercise would be relatively meaningless. Accordingly, I have adopted the convention that all new spending counts against the $10 billion and $40 billion ceilings except for those program expansions that can be paid for by offsetting reductions made within the same program or the same feature of the tax code.

Robert Greenstein is executive director of the Center on Budget and Policy Priorities.

Uses for $40 Billion

I have divided my suggestions for using $40 billion into three components: (1) major initiatives, which account for about $35 billion; (2) smaller elements, accounting for about $5 billion; and (3) proposals to restructure programs without increasing their costs.

Major Initiatives

The central challenge is to fashion plans that can provide stronger income support to low-income families with children while avoiding the political and substantive pitfalls of the welfare system. To accomplish this aim entails beginning partially to replace the current system with alternative supports that bolster rather than conflict with the values of work, family, and parental responsibility.

In this vein, I would undertake a major overhaul of the child support system, with much stricter procedures for establishing paternity and collecting child support, coupled with the establishment of child support assurance. Irwin Garfinkel's paper in this volume provides a more detailed discussion of how such a revised system of child support would function and of its advantages. I do not have an exact price tag for this initiative, but Garfinkel's analysis suggests that its costs may be relatively modest, certainly less than a third of the $35 billion that I have reserved for major initiatives. A significant part of the cost of boosting child support payments will either be borne by absent parents (through increases in collections of child support) or be offset through reductions in welfare benefits.

Some proposals for child support enforcement and assurance include work requirements, training programs, and ultimately public service jobs for absent fathers who have no income and cannot pay child support. Inclusion of such provisions for absent parents who are consistently unable to meet their child support obligations is wise. They would, however, add to the cost of the changes in child support proposed here, at least in the short run.

My second major initiative is to convert the personal exemption for children into a refundable children's credit. This shift was recommended on a unanimous bipartisan basis by the National Commission on Children. Such a credit would substantially ease child poverty while making the tax code more progressive. In addition, it would lessen the disincentives to work and to marry that are present in the current welfare system; the credit would not decline if a poor family secured work or if a single parent married. The United States stands virtually alone among western industrialized nations in lacking a children's credit or allowance, and this lack is one reason that our child poverty rates dwarf those in western Europe and Canada.[1]

The National Commission on Children recommended the establishment of a $1,000 credit for each child. I would set the credit somewhat lower—at about $700—because at $1,000, the credit would consume the entire $40 billion. If it were $700, families with children in the zero, 15 percent, and 28 percent income tax brackets would all receive a credit worth more than the current personal exemption. To set the credit *below* the value of the personal exemption in the 28 percent tax bracket would make it impossible to enact.

If further trimming proved necessary to fit the child tax credit within the $40 billion ceiling, I would shave the age of the children covered by the credit to below eighteen. I would pay for the children's credit by increasing tax rates on upper-income families or by broadening the income tax base. (Under the conventions I have established, the full cost of converting the exemption to a credit still counts against the $40 billion limit.)

The last major initiative would be a substantial expansion of housing certificates and vouchers for poor households (probably in the $5 billion to $8 billion range). Some readers may ask: Why do that? Why not just provide cash transfers? There are several elements to my answer. If all of the $40 billion were spent on universal cash programs such as child support assurance and children's credits, the benefits at the bottom of the income scale would not be so large as I would like. A mixture of universal and targeted programs is necessary to achieve a substantial improvement in the living conditions of poor children and their families.

Second, universal cash assistance programs that spread their benefits broadly will be insufficient, by themselves, to address adequately the burden of high housing costs borne by many poor families. Data from the American Housing Survey show that in 1989, the peak year of the economic recovery, over half of all poor renter households spent more than 50 percent of their incomes for housing. (Among poor renters not receiving a government housing subsidy, nearly three-fourths paid more than 50 percent of their income for housing.) Under federal standards established during the Reagan Administration, housing is considered affordable for a low-income household if it does not consume more than 30 *percent* of income. An increase in housing certificates and vouchers concentrates resources on low-income families with high housing costs.

---

1. McFate (1991); Hanratty and Blank (1990).

In addition, findings from the Gautreaux experiment in Chicago suggest that enabling poor families to move from poor inner-city areas into suburban neighborhoods increases employment and educational attainment.[2] Currently, many poor families can find affordable housing only in dangerous, crime-ridden, or otherwise undesirable neighborhoods; living in such areas may have adverse effects on themselves and their children. Providing portable housing subsidies through certificates and vouchers, helping to find available housing in areas with stronger employment and educational opportunities, and counseling on the advantages of moving to such locations should enable more of these families to move to other neighborhoods.

Other data from the American Housing Survey underscore the need for a major initiative in this area. In 1970, there were 400,000 more low-rent housing units than low-income renters. By 1989, there were *4.1 million fewer* low-rent units than low-income renters.[3]

Smaller Program Improvements and Enhancements

To the three major initiatives—child support enforcement and assurance, conversion of the personal exemption for children into a refundable credit, and substantial expansion of tenant-based housing assistance—I would add about $5 billion in smaller improvements to certain programs. These include improvements in food stamps, aid to families with dependent children, the dependent care tax credit, the women, infants, and children program, and the HOME program.

The food stamp program treats the elderly and the disabled with heavy housing costs differently from, and more favorably than, families with children with such burdens. In calculating income for purposes of assigning food stamp benefits, households receive a deduction for the amount that housing costs exceed 50 percent of net income. But for households of the nonelderly and able-bodied, there is an artificial cap on the amount that can be deducted. (During fiscal year 1992, it is $194 a month.) As a result, some of the funds spent on rent by nonelderly families with heavy housing cost burdens are assumed to be available for

---

2. Rosenbaum and Popkin (1991); Kaufman and Rosenbaum (1991).

3. Low-income renters are defined here as renter households with incomes below $10,000 in 1989 dollars. Low-rent units are those for which rent and utility costs do not exceed $250 a month in 1989 dollars, or 30 percent of a $10,000 income. All data on low-rent units and low-income renters are from the American Housing Survey, conducted by the Census Bureau for the U.S. Department of Housing and Urban Development. For further analysis of these matters, see Lazere and others (1991).

food purchases; and so the food stamp benefits that these families receive are too low.

The shelter deduction should be made uniform, with nonelderly and able-bodied families treated in the same manner as the elderly and disabled. Legislation making this and other useful improvements in the food stamp program, at an ultimate cost of about $1.5 billion per year, passed the House of Representatives in August 1990 by a vote of 336 to 83. It later died in the budget summit that year. This legislation is primarily targeted on poor families with children, who would receive over 90 percent of the benefits in the package.

In aid to families with dependent children (AFDC), several steps could be taken. The limit on assets should be modified. The limit is now so low—$1,000 in countable assets—that if you accumulate assets to launch a personal business or to make a security deposit and pay the first month's rent so you can move out of a housing project or a dangerous neighborhood, you are removed from the AFDC program.

In addition, the penalties the AFDC program imposes on work and marriage should be eased. Such changes would allow working families to retain more of their earnings, remove eligibility restrictions imposed solely on two-parent families, and modify rules on the treatment of income from step-parents.[4]

I would also recommend a few other improvements with modest costs. The child care tax credit should be made refundable, and the percentage of child care expenses eligible for the credit should be raised for families with low incomes. The current nonrefundable credit is a government child care subsidy, delivered through the tax code, that shuts out low-income families and confers most of its benefits on those in the middle and upper parts of the income spectrum.[5] I would offset part of the cost of this expansion by phasing down the credit—from 20 percent of covered child care costs to 10 percent—for those with higher incomes. (The credit is already phased down from 30 percent of covered costs to 20 percent as family income rises from $10,000 to $28,000. It could be phased down from 20 percent to 10 percent in, say, the $80,000 to $100,000 range.)

Another improvement would be to fund fully, by fiscal year 1996, the special supplemental food program for women, infants, and children, which provides highly nutritious foods to low-income pregnant women, infants, and young children at nutritional risk. This change

---

4. Greenberg (1992).

5. Because the credit is not refundable, low-income working families that do not earn enough to owe income tax receive no benefit from it, while near-poor families with small income tax liabilities receive only a partial credit.

would mean that all eligible applicants could be served. It would cost a little more than $1 billion a year.

Lastly, I would fund HOME, the block grant program that provides funds for low-income housing to state and local governments, at the full $2 billion authorized in the National Affordable Housing Act. (This proposal entails a $500 million increase.) Although the thrust in the housing area should be more certificates and vouchers, the HOME block grant program enables state and local governments to use funds for low-income housing construction and rehabilitation in areas with tight housing markets.

No-Cost Restructuring

I would restructure two current programs—the earned income tax credit (EITC) and unemployment insurance—without increasing their costs. The EITC has grown too complex and should be simplified. I would eliminate the two supplemental credits added in 1990—the supplement for young children and the health insurance credit. I would also drop the adjustment for family size, which would be unnecessary if a refundable children's credit were enacted. I would then plow the savings from eliminating these three provisions into an enlargement of the basic EITC.

In the case of unemployment insurance (UI), two permanent, structural reforms are needed: shoring up the extended benefits program, so those benefits are more readily available in states with high unemployment, and easing some of the more severe rules by which states restrict access to regular unemployment insurance benefits. UI serves a much smaller proportion of the jobless population now than in the past. The added costs could be fully financed through raising the UI taxable wage base to the same level as that for Social Security and sharply reducing the UI tax rate. This change would both make the UI tax more progressive and pay for the increases in UI benefits.[6]

How to Use $10 Billion

If $10 billion in new funds were available rather than $40 billion—a more likely scenario—major changes in this package of recommendations would be needed. First, I would drop the refundable children's credit, the single most costly item in the $40 billion package.

---

6. Shapiro and Nichols (1992). See also the papers by Robert H. Topel, Gary Burtless, and Richard W. McHugh in Van de Water (1992).

It is not possible to establish a meaningful children's credit within a $10 billion constraint. Politically, it is highly unlikely that the personal exemption could be converted into a refundable credit if the credit were set lower than the value of the personal exemption for taxpayers in the 28 percent tax bracket. And setting the credit at this level would cost significantly more than $10 billion a year.

It would be possible to establish a children's credit for $10 billion a year if the personal exemption remained untouched and the credit were set at about $200 or $250 per child. That amount, however, is too modest to make any real difference (it equals $4 to $5 per child per week), and virtually all of the $10 billion would be consumed by this one proposal.

Under the $10 billion option, I would retain the child support enforcement and assurance initiative (though it would probably have to be modified to reduce its cost), and I would retain (but significantly scale back) the increase in tenant-based housing assistance. I would also include increases in food stamps and AFDC, but more modest than those I suggested under the $40 billion option. I would make the child care credit refundable but would not increase the benefits the credit provides, and I would phase the credit out—rather than down—for high-income taxpayers. I would continue to seek funding increases for WIC.

I would restructure the earned income tax credit, but in a manner different from that I suggested under the $40 billion option. In the absence of a refundable children's tax credit, the EITC adjustment for family size should be retained and enlarged. Census data analyzed by the Center on Budget and Policy Priorities indicate that about 60 percent of all children in poor working families live in families with three or more children. Accordingly, I would create a third tier in the EITC for families with three or more children and set the credit rate for these families at 29 percent or 30 percent (instead of the current 25 percent for families with two or more children).

I would offset the cost of expanding the EITC by eliminating the two new supplemental credits, the health insurance credit and the supplement for young children. These two accomplish little while greatly complicating the EITC. An enhanced adjustment for family size represents sounder policy. If it were not politically feasible to eliminate both supplemental credits, I would cover the remainder of the cost of expanding the adjustment by slightly reducing the rate of the EITC for families with one child.

Lastly, I would retain the same cost-neutral changes in the unemployment insurance program as under the $40 billion option.

References

Greenberg, Mark. Testimony before the U.S. House of Representatives, Select Committee on Hunger, Domestic Task Force, April 9, 1992.

Hanratty, Maria J., and Rebecca M. Blank. *Down and Out in North America: Recent Trends in Poverty Rates in the U.S. and Canada.* Cambridge: National Bureau of Economic Research, 1990.

Kaufman, Julie E., and James E. Rosenbaum. *The Education and Employment of Low-Income Black Youth in White Suburbs.* Evanston, IL: Center for Urban Affairs and Policy Research, Northwestern University, 1991.

Lazere, Edward B., Paul A. Leonard, Cushing N. Dolbeare, and Barry Zigas. *A Place to Call Home: The Low Income Housing Crisis Continues.* Washington: Center on Budget and Policy Priorities and Low Income Housing Information Service, 1991.

McFate, Katherine. *Poverty, Inequality, and the Crisis of Social Policy: Summary of Findings.* Washington: Joint Center for Political and Economic Studies, 1991.

Rosenbaum, James E., and Susan J. Popkin. "Employment and Earnings of Low-Income Blacks Who Move to Middle-Class Suburbs," in Christopher Jencks and Paul E. Peterson, eds., *The Urban Underclass.* Washington: Brookings Institution, 1991.

Shapiro, Isaac, and Marion Nichols. *Far From Fixed: An Analysis of the Unemployment Insurance System.* Washington: Center on Budget and Policy Priorities, 1992.

Van de Water, Paul N., ed. *Social Insurance Issues for the Nineties: Proceedings of the Third Conference of the National Academy of Social Insurance.* Dubuque, IA: Kendall-Hunt, 1992.

WHAT COULD $10 BILLION OR $40 BILLION DO FOR CHILDREN? ANOTHER VIEW

Rudolph G. Penner

W hen Henry Aaron asked me to prepare this paper, I thought there were two problems. First of all, I do not know much about children's programs. That is not a serious barrier, however, because I worked for the Congress for four years, and I can certainly discourse briefly on a topic about which I know virtually nothing.

The second barrier is more serious. I am an old budget hand, and the thought of $10 billion or $40 billion magically becoming available is quite strange to a budget person. We are used to $10 billion or $40 billion disappearing magically, but rarely do such sums materialize out of nothing.

This issue is serious enough that it warrants a little discussion. We should briefly consider the real world before entering the wish world. This is a time when the two political parties are competing to see which can give away more resources to the middle class. These are resources that we do not have.

The numbers in the President's 1993 budget are sobering. The budget contains a substantial peace dividend—perhaps not so big as the one we will eventually get but still a very substantial one. The budget

Rudolph G. Penner, currently director of economic studies at KPMG Peat Marwick, is a former director of the Congressional Budget Office.

also assumes an economic growth rate that is higher than we can expect in the very long run, and that is quite appropriate, given that we are coming out of a recession. It constrains entitlement and discretionary spending enough to provoke howls of anguish. Yes, it does have some tax cuts, but they are fairly trivial. Even so, the projected deficits are large.

So, it is a cold, hard world out there. It is not necessarily a world in which nothing will be available for children, but it is a world in which our exercise here could truly be called academic.

Before deciding where to spend an extra $10 billion or $40 billion, we must also give thought to where the money will come from because many of the ways of getting money could be detrimental to children. Maybe you could minimize the impact on children by hitting the elderly up one way or another, say, by taxing Social Security benefits as though they were regular pension income. Doing that would raise about $20 billion. Alternatively, you could tax the subsidy value of Medicare or something of that sort. But the House Ways and Means Committees's *Green Book* tells me that Social Security is in fact the biggest single children's program going, in that the very small percentage of that huge program that goes to children totals more than most programs explicitly targeted on children. So, it would be very difficult to raise the money by taxing those benefits without doing some damage to children.

Establishing Criteria

I assume that the focus of this exercise is poor children, rather than all children. When it comes to helping *all* children, it seems to me, the standard of comparison for any program is deficit reduction. The benefits from deficit reduction are substantial, but they will take so long to accrue that they will mainly benefit our children.

Defining the problem as improving the lot of poor children, here are some criteria for deciding where extra money should be spent. Mark Twain once said, "All generalizations are wrong, including this one." That is the spirit in which I put forth the following generalizations.

First, the federal government is most efficient when it simply gives money away. That it does extremely well.

Second, money given to parents will improve the life of their children, although there will be some leakage. That is not a proposition that is universally believed, but I suspect that most of the participants in this conference believe it.

Third, money can be channeled to parents most effectively through the tax system or existing welfare system, rather than by inventing new programs. I do not mean to rule out comprehensive reform, but I think that laying new programs on top of the current hodge-podge will complicate analysis of the interactions among programs and of the cumulative value of various incentives and disincentives.

Fourth, the federal government is least efficient when it tries to stimulate the delivery of services at the state or local level using narrow, categorical grants. This is not to say that categorical grants should never be made, only that I regard them with a good deal of skepticism. Of course, one of the most popular programs—Head Start—is of this type. Here, I do not know enough to evaluate the evaluators. I do not really know whether it is the exception to the rule or is being oversold.

Changes in Taxes

On the tax side, one of my favorite programs is the earned income tax credit (EITC). Changes to the EITC in 1990 made it very complex. The rate of the credit was raised, as was the rate of the phase out. Also, an adjustment for family size was added. The result of these and other reforms was an extraordinarily complicated tax schedule. You almost have to be a certified public accountant to figure it out.

Even apart from these complexities, the EITC has some severe disadvantages. It raises the disincentive to work over the range of incomes in which it is being phased out. Moreover, it may not deliver the money when it is needed because it typically comes in a lump sum after tax returns are filed. The law provides for negative withholding, but I gather that employers are reluctant to participate. Despite all of these problems, I would spend more on the EITC if money were available. It is a good way of offsetting some of the work disincentives at the very bottom of the income scale.

In reforming and expanding the earned income tax credit, its relation to the number of children could be improved. A third tier could be introduced for families with three or more children, as Bob Greenstein suggested in his $10 billion option. You could vary the maximum credit, as well.

Is the EITC better than a refundable tax credit for each child? You could make them almost identical, and you could phase out a refundable tax credit fairly quickly as income rises. But I prefer linking the subsidy to earnings to demonstrate concern for stimulating work effort.

In improving the EITC, one faces the traditional welfare dilemma of making it sufficiently generous at the bottom while not discouraging work in the phase-out range or letting costs get out of control. I would spend some money to reduce the phase-out rate toward the 10 percent that existed in prior law. But the problem is that you then have a subsidy that extends far up the income distribution; under my proposal, undoubtedly, some credit would still linger for incomes over $30,000 for larger families. Some people might find that objectionable.

Changes in Spending

On the spending side, I believe it is time to make aid to families with dependent children more generous. We have been cutting it rapidly in real terms by not keeping grants up with inflation. So, I would increase the federal share of costs to encourage states to be more generous. I would not, however, mandate such increases on top of the already oppressively long list of mandates on state and local governments. I would only increase the federal share and hope for the best.

I would also relax the asset test for AFDC. Like the asset test for supplemental security income, it is extraordinarily low and totally unrealistic. Bob Greenstein has eloquently stated the reasons for relaxing it. Surely you want to allow a person enough money, as he said, to make a security deposit on an apartment, to take a course, or to buy a share in a taxicab.

Child support has had many advocates at this conference, and I would count myself among them. I would certainly reduce AFDC's current implicit tax of 100 percent on child support payments greater than $50 a month. This change would not only increase the income of AFDC mothers but would also give fathers a sense of responsibility for their children and for the economic consequences of their actions. It would also make fathers feel that their payments actually help their children instead of going to a welfare agency. Finally, I wish that we could rely less on the courts for running the child support system, perhaps by creating some sort of administrative law procedure.

I probably have not spent my allowance of $10 billion, let alone $40 billion, on my candidates for additional budget dollars. But, as an old budget person, my heart was not in the $40 billion. It is just incomprehensible that so much money should become available; so I must retire from the game.

COMMENTS

Allan C. Carlson

Rudolph Penner made his operating assumptions fairly explicit. Robert Greenstein's assumptions were not presented so explicitly, but they were clear nonetheless. I, too, want to lay out my assumptions at the start.

First, the American welfare state, although less comprehensive than its western European counterparts, may be lumbering toward the same sort of crisis that bedevils European social democracies: swollen budget deficits, retarded capital formation, growing pressure on public services, deterioration of family life as household units surrender their remaining functions to collective agencies, transfer of wealth and resources from the young to the old, loss of belief among young adults that the system is fair and sustainable, and horror stories spawned by the government's rationing of health services.

Second, the government should not engage in the engineering of lifestyles, in which it conditions child-related benefits on adherence to a few distinct patterns of correct behavior.

Third, the existing system of federal child welfare—aid to families with dependent children, food stamps, and the child-care tax credit—is overly complicated and resistant to reform. It needs to be simplified and reworked to remove the disincentives toward marriage and work that now exist.

Allan C. Carlson is president of the Rockford Institute.

Fourth, people should be treated as responsible adults who are able to make their own choices. Therefore, if and when the state provides benefits, cash is better than in-kind benefits.

Fifth, the primary governmental responsibility for interacting with families and meeting social needs should reside with the states and localities.

Finally, my central goal is the reconstruction of more autonomous free-standing family units, operating on the principle, "From each according to his or her ability, to each according to his or her need."

A Refundable Tax Credit for Children

Although my assumptions may be somewhat different from those of Greenstein and Penner, they lead me to agree with their emphasis on tax credits, although I would carry the idea further than either of them. As a member of the National Commission on Children, I enthusiastically supported its principal recommendation of substituting a $1,000 refundable, indexed tax credit per child for the personal exemption for children. It has a price tag of $40 billion, and that is how I would spend my $40 billion.

Why do I support the tax credit? One reason is that families with children have been the big losers during the last three decades of federal income redistribution.

Eugene Steuerle's justly famed work of ten years ago provided dramatic examples of the erosion in the value of the personal exemption.[1] For instance, between 1960 and the early 1980s, single persons and childless couples saw no significant change in the net federal income tax rate they faced, but a married couple with four children experienced a staggering 223 percent increase in its income tax rate.

The same years were marked by a dramatic increase in the payroll taxes for Social Security and Medicare, which also fell disproportionately on young families with children. Although this is an oversimplification, it still appears that the Great Society, the War on Poverty, and the war in Indochina were financed primarily by families raising children.

Of course, some steps have been taken to reduce the problem, notably the Tax Reform Act of 1986, which increased the personal exemption and indexed it. But this is insufficient. A credit of $1,000 per child would increase by at least one-third the tax relief granted parents raising children.

---

1. Steuerle (1984).

An Opportunity for Welfare Reform

The child credit would not only provide tax relief but would also be refundable. Here I part company with the majority of the National Commission on Children and possibly with Greenstein and Penner. If the refundable credit were to be simply an add-on to existing federal welfare benefits, then I would oppose refundability. But if it is seen as an opportunity for welfare reform, then many possibilities open up.

To begin with, I would use the refundable tax credit to reduce the federal contributions to AFDC and food stamps. Both programs are means-tested and thus place the recipients in the hands of bureaucratic decisionmakers. They both impose a tax on paid labor and so discourage moves toward independence. And AFDC contains disincentives to marriage that various reforms over the decades have not fully eliminated. A universal refundable tax credit, in contrast, does not tax work. It easily and smoothly transfers over from welfare benefit to tax relief. Its effect on incentives to marry is unclear, but I am willing to bet that it would be more supportive than the existing welfare structure.

With a child credit, I would also eliminate or fold in the child-care tax credit. This benefit goes disproportionately to the relatively well off and suffers from another basic problem. It gives indirect aid to those parents who hire an institution or another person to care for their children but gives nothing to parents who struggle to provide care for their own children, be it through job sharing, working different shifts, or giving up a second income in order to keep one parent at home. It is a classic case of federal lifestyle engineering, which should be rolled into a unified refundable credit.

If the credit's value could be raised to, say, $1,500 per child or even higher, then one might even consider rolling the earned income tax credit into the unified child credit. Despite all of its virtues, the earned income tax credit remains a cumbersome and underutilized form of tax relief and welfare supplementation. A unified credit would, at least, have the virtue of simplicity.

In the end, a universal refundable child credit would become an American version of a child allowance, but a version with many distinctions. For most Americans, it would take the form of tax relief, not a cash benefit. It would require neither a new government agency nor an army of social investigators. It would treat recipients as responsible adults and could end some troubled experiments in workfare. It would transfer real power and choices from collective structures to the family.

Finally, a refundable child credit would, for the first time, give rich families with children and poor families with children a vested interest in each other. When the credit goes up, both benefit. The bias against children in a system in which children do not vote would be blunted. The credit would contribute to the kind of social solidarity that must undergird any successful system of security for America's children.

Reference

Steuerle, C. Eugene. "The Tax Treatment of Households of Different Size," in Rudolph G. Penner, ed., *Taxing the Family*. Washington: American Enterprise Institute, 1984.

COMMENTS

Olivia Golden

Because we cannot afford *not* to reduce child poverty, we should adopt the social insurance framework that Bob Greenstein has proposed. In fact, I favor an even broader range of social insurance programs than he suggests.

Children's income security has never been shakier. One in five children is poor, and the younger a child is, the more likely he or she is to be poor. Almost one in four children in the crucial developmental years before age six is poor. About 40 percent of children in young families—by which we don't mean families headed by teens but families headed by people under age 30—are poor.

As Mary Jo Bane indicates in her paper, the connection between low incomes and bad outcomes is blurry, but it is real. A variety of evidence suggests that poverty in childhood is linked to poor health, inadequate nutrition, limited educational achievement, a greater likelihood of teen pregnancy and parenthood, and worse outcomes throughout life. By not reducing poverty among families with children, the United States thus not only is sacrificing many of our children but also is making some frightening choices about the future.

What does that imply for spending $40 billion? I would not take the approach of Rudy Penner, who tried to identify what could be enacted in today's climate and couldn't come up with $40 billion worth of programs. Instead, we must convince people that the task is urgent, change the political climate, and make spending $40 billion possible.

Olivia Golden is director of programs and policy for the Children's Defense Fund.

We should begin by looking for successes. I find two. One is the American Social Security system, which has halved poverty rates for the elderly. Another is the institutions that have allowed European nations that we regard as our peers and with whom we compete to have child poverty rates no more than half ours.

A Striking Comparison

For the past few years, I have taught a course in family policy at the Kennedy School at Harvard University. The course typically has many foreign students. It also has many people who are returning to school after several years, including parents. Last year, in the class on parental leave, I noted a striking comparison.

The American parents in the course were generally well educated and well off, and they usually had managed to negotiate some parental leave with their employer. But they typically felt that they were at fault when they did so. "I had to make a deal with my employer," they said. "My coworkers were irritated that they were going to have to pick up my work and thought I was getting something that wasn't fair. I ended up getting only a month or two of parental leave."

In sharp contrast was the response of an Israeli student, who was well up in the civil service and had two young children. She had received six months of paid leave when her children were born—roughly typical of western nations other than the United States. None of the American students had managed to finagle that much, even though they were an elite group. She said that what stunned her about the American students' reports of their experiences was not so much the results but the underlying assumptions about what was fair. Here, the burden was on the individual parents to negotiate a deal in which other people did them a favor. In her country, she could take the six months of paid leave for granted. She knew she was eligible for it and didn't have to worry about it. The assumption was that all citizens benefit from enabling parents to care for their children.

Social Insurance for Children

Bearing and nurturing children is not a bad choice that a few people make. It is a choice that many people make. And it is a choice that can be made easier by supportive social policies. Together, we can insure parents against their individual burdens and provide for the nurture of all children.

That is what the social insurance approach to raising family incomes is about. It is not only about how today's single mother combines work and welfare, gets her ex-husband to pay child support on time, and copes with existing institutions. It is about designing new institutions to help people nurture children and support them.

What about spending $40 billion? I agree with Bob Greenstein's principle that if you can't get everything you want, you should make a beginning on several initiatives, rather than spend everything on a single one. One way to make a beginning would be to focus first on young children. For example, you could try to eliminate poverty among families with children under age three, to show that it can be done.

Countries that employ the social insurance approach do not have a single big program. They mix child allowances, housing allowances, guaranteed child support, and paid parental leave. In fact, I would add paid leave to Bob Greenstein's package; six months of paid parental leave would cost about $5 billion a year, according to the Panel on Child Care Policy of the National Research Council. Such a mix, as Allan Carlson said, can give poor families and rich families a stake in the same set of programs, and I think it will work here, as it has abroad.

The social insurance approach not only is the only one that can improve dramatically the well-being of the bottom quarter of families. It also sends the right signals.

Welfare sends the signal that poverty is about bad choices by individual women. But child support assurance is about the need for men, as well as women, to invest in their children's upbringing. Paid parental leave is about society's interest in helping families nurture children with time as well as money. Refundable tax credits or children's allowances send a message about our common stake in the nurturing and the upbringing of children.

COMMENTS

Wendell E. Primus

I n his State of the Union address for 1992, President Bush said that Americans are the most generous people on earth. He also said that when able-bodied people receive government assistance, they have responsibilities to the taxpayer—responsibilities to seek work, education, or job training; to get their lives in order; to hold their families together and refrain from having children out of wedlock; and to obey the law. It is very hard to argue with those principles.

But our social institutions should send signals that comport with those principles, and our present welfare system doesn't do that. If we want work, we shouldn't put marginal tax rates of 70, 80, or 90 percent on earnings. If we want people to get married, we shouldn't penalize them as heavily as we do. If we want fathers to pay child support, we shouldn't put 100 percent marginal tax rates on child support payments.

Meeting these concerns, I believe, requires fundamental changes in our system of welfare. Currently, about one-fourth of all children are born out of wedlock. Experts estimate that more than half of all children born today will be eligible for child support at some time before they reach age 18. These trends are even more staggering when you take into account the dismal record of child support in this country. Many noncustodial parents fail to pay their child support obligations. Only 60 percent of noncustodial fathers have a legal obligation to pay child support. Of those fathers, only half pay the full amount, and 24 percent pay nothing. Thus, more than half of all families with children potentially eligible for support receive nothing.

Wendell E. Primus is the chief economist for the House Committee on Ways and Means and staff director of its Subcommittee on Human Resources.

Without consistent and timely child support payments, many middle-income families have difficulty meeting basic needs, and lower-income parents and their children are often pushed into poverty. Welfare has picked up the pieces where noncustodial parents have failed to provide support. But welfare comes at a cost to taxpayers, who must pay the bill, and to recipients, who suffer the stigma of public assistance and severe disincentives to work. This country can no longer afford to let the noncustodial parents off the hook.

The staff of the Subcommittee on Human Resources of the Committee on Ways and Means has been drafting a child support enforcement and assurance proposal under the direction of its chairman, Congressman Thomas J. Downey (D-NY). Parental responsibility demands enforcement of child support obligations. And society's responsibility for helping low-income children requires that custodial parents no longer be penalized by the refusal of noncustodial parents to pay support. The two must go hand in hand.

Five key elements must be addressed in reforming the child support system: the establishment of paternity, the establishment of child support orders, the enforcement of child support, job training and education for noncustodial parents who are unable to pay support, and an assured child support benefit.

The establishment of paternity should be completely decoupled from the welfare system. A child has a right to know who his or her biological father is for many reasons. Children who do not have paternity established lose opportunities to receive a range of benefits including Social Security, military allotments, workers' compensation, health insurance, and inheritance. Such children also forgo noneconomic benefits, such as information on the family's medical and genetic history and the psychological value of knowing the identity of one's father. Mothers must be encouraged to identify the alleged father of their children, although reasonable people will differ on what benefits should be denied if a mother doesn't cooperate.

Once paternity is established, more must be done to order the noncustodial parent to pay child support. Because of widespread inconsistency in the determination of awards across state lines, as well as frequent changes in the earnings of both parents, federal guidelines must be established for setting child support awards, and those awards must be updated periodically to reflect both parents' current ability to pay child support.

To ensure that child support payments are effectively collected and enforced, the entire child support system must undergo fundamental change. Federal collection and enforcement through the Internal Revenue Service or a new agency with similar powers is needed to improve the dismal collection and enforcement records of the states. A significant barrier to effective enforcement today is raised by the difficulty in enforcing interstate cases, which make up almost a third of all child support cases. A federalized system would eliminate the current difficulties in enforcing cases that are caught between the bureaucracies of several states. Furthermore, the use of the IRS and the employer wage-withholding system for collection and enforcement would send a strong message to noncustodial parents and the public at large about the seriousness of child support obligations. It is critical that child support obligations be enforced by the IRS to the same degree as income taxes due to the federal government.

More attention must be focused on the noncustodial parent's role in the child support system. The Job Opportunities and Basic Skills Training program established under the Family Support Act of 1988 helps welfare mothers to work their way off welfare by making them self-sufficient. But the current system does nothing to address the needs of fathers. A JOBS program targeted on noncustodial parents would recognize that many parents lack the human capital to support a family adequately. Noncustodial parents who refuse to pay support and accumulate arrearages would be required to participate substantially in workfare and job search activities. These strict requirements could deter noncustodial parents both from gaming the system by making payments under the table and from failing to disclose earned income.

A minimum assured benefit should be provided to children whose noncustodial parents fail to pay their child support obligations. The assured benefit accomplishes several goals. First, it simultaneously provides economic security to families with children and reduces welfare receipt. Second, because the benefit does not decrease as earnings rise, it makes it economically viable for a mother to leave welfare and return to work, thereby eliminating the strong work disincentives inherent in the current welfare system.

Finally, in addition to assuring child support, we need to spend more on other programs targeted on children. A portion of the peace dividend should be devoted to investments in human capital, such as Head Start, WIC, immunization, reductions in infant mortality, and help for children who are abused or neglected by their parents.

We are considering taking a $99 billion gamble on reducing the taxation of capital gains: If there is no increase in their realization, an exclusion of 45 percent of capital gains from taxation will cost $99 billion, according to the Treasury's estimates. If we are willing to make that kind of wager for economic growth, I think we can afford to invest a similar sum in our children—an investment that will also improve the competitiveness of our economy.

COMMENTS

Margaret C. Simms

W hat do children need most? Both Bob Greenstein and Rudy Penner said that children need more money. Greenstein chose to focus on Function 600 in the federal budget, and within that function he recommended additional income transfers, nutrition assistance, and housing allowances. Penner, too, argued that giving families more money is the most effective means of dealing with children's problems. Neither Greenstein nor Penner, however, made clear his primary goal. Is it to lift the greatest number of children out of poverty? Or is it to narrow the poverty gap by focusing resources on the poorest of the poor? Greenstein seemed to lean in the direction of targeting the very poor. But I am not sure that the programs he selected would achieve this objective.

Consider, for example, child support enforcement, which seems to be very popular at this conference. How many dollars that system generates depends upon the resources of the noncustodial parent. In many families, as Irv Garfinkel noted, the earnings of the noncustodial parent are likely to be too low to lift his children out of poverty, even if he makes reasonable child support payments. Therefore, if we want to invest in children by improving their parents' ability to support them, we should provide training and jobs not only for welfare mothers but also for absent fathers. This step is likely to do more to increase the incomes of the poorest of the poor than some of the other programs that Greenstein and Penner suggested. Although Greenstein noted the

---

Margaret C. Simms is director of research programs at the Joint Center for Political and Economic Studies.

potential benefits of training and jobs, he did not include them in his recommendations.

Several participants in this conference have suggested that a family's AFDC benefits should not be reduced by increases in child support payments. I concur with that suggestion and would allocate a portion of the $40 billion to cover the costs of maintaining AFDC benefits to such families. Additional child support payments should not only save public dollars but also increase the income of the child's family. Penner included this proposal in his package, but Greenstein did not.

I have a couple of reservations about Greenstein's proposal to spend an additional $5 billion to $8 billion on housing allowances. Not that I don't think housing is a serious problem, but it is not clear to me how far the coverage of the programs could be increased with that sum of money. If we couldn't extend housing assistance to all of the poor, would it be the poorest of the poor who would benefit?

Greenstein's and Penner's proposals assume implicitly that the market is an effective mechanism for fulfilling children's needs. They assume, for example, that if children lack decent housing, seeing that their parents have more money will enable them to obtain decent housing in safe neighborhoods with good schools. But I question whether money solves all of the problems of the children that I, at least, am interested in. The market may not supply the needed services—for example, good day care or affordable housing—and the parents may not spend the additional money on the services that children need most.

PART III

••• ◉ •••

RETOOLING FOR CHILDREN'S HEALTH SECURITY

HEALTH CARE REFORM: WHAT'S IN IT FOR MOTHERS AND CHILDREN?

Sarah S. Brown

T he debate about reforming the U.S. health care system has inten- sified over the last several years. It seems increasingly likely that within its next few sessions, the Congress will pass a major bill to alter fundamentally the financing of the health care system. The final legislation, however, may not adequately reflect the special needs of pregnant women and young children. One of the main reasons for this concern is that the risk-based insurance model that is the cornerstone of most health care financing plans tends to ignore the primary and pre- ventive care so important to this population. Moreover, many of the most important challenges in maternal and child health have little to do with expanding health insurance.

A Pessimistic Scenario

When I am in a pessimistic mood about health care reform, I envision the following scenario. One morning, the *New York Times* carries a banner headline reading "President Signs Comprehensive Health Care Reform Bill." A picture on the front page shows the

Sarah S. Brown is senior study director for the National Forum on the Future of Children and Families, a joint project of the Institute of Medicine and the National Research Council.

President, surrounded by a group of beaming congressional leaders from both parties, signing the bill in the White House rose garden.

Over the next few days, the commentary about the 515-page bill is largely favorable. The new law helps small and new businesses purchase health insurance for their employees. It improves the tax treatment of the health insurance premiums paid by self-employed people. It brings more uniformity to Medicaid and increases its reimbursement rates, especially those for inner-city hospitals that care for a disproportionate number of very sick and uninsured patients.

In the following months, however, as I continue my work as an advocate for maternal and child health in the District of Columbia, I find that the new law has left many problems unsolved and has created several new ones. D.C. General Hospital remains unable to hire a perinatologist. The community health center in Anacostia is still unable to find enough physicians to staff its prenatal clinics, and it cancels the Saturday clinic because of medical liability problems. And the paperwork required to provide adequate care to a handicapped, poor child in the District has grown from outrageous to simply impossible.

The last of these developments is due to a Byzantine chain of unintended effects. Instead of a poor child's care being financed entirely by Medicaid, which was difficult enough, there are now two financing schemes: the new public plan, which replaced much of Medicaid, and Medicaid, which still pays for those benefits not provided by the new public plan. For the handicapped child, many key services such as care coordination and speech therapy are not covered by the new public plan but are available only through an even more turgid means-tested program. Finally, because the providers who take Medicaid patients are not the same as those who take patients under the new public plan, the child and her family must now visit even more providers all over town to stitch together needed care.

Even when these problems begin to be documented and described around the country, I fantasize, advocates find virtually no receptivity to their claims. Policymakers are exhausted from developing the recent legislation. They are in a state of terminal compassion fatigue; they tell the advocates that health care reform is finished as an issue for at least ten years and that they should occupy themselves with some other problem, such as juvenile justice.

This scenario is, of course, of my own making; but it was gratifying to find that it was shared, in part, by colleagues at the National Academy of Sciences. Under the Academy's auspices, a group of us participated in several workshops in mid-1991 to consider the place of maternal and child health in health care reform. Our group concluded that while children's issues are now in vogue, the special health care problems of children and pregnant women may still be overlooked. Although all Americans are caught up in a chaotic health care system that shows increasing strain, children have a right to special attention, in part because of the many differences between their health needs and those of adults, but also because of their inability to be their own advocates. Thus the National Academy of Sciences decided to develop a monograph discussing the important health policy issues presented by children and pregnant women that any major proposal for health care reform should address. The resulting document, *Including Children and Pregnant Women in Health Care Reform,* forms the basis of my paper.

Health Care Needs of Mothers and Children

What issues need to be faced squarely in a health care reform bill if the health of children and pregnant women is to be enhanced? The National Academy of Sciences study identified eleven issues, of which I will discuss seven.

Providing Access to Health Insurance and Health Care

First, all children and pregnant women should have access to an affordable and continuous source of payment for health care—typically, health insurance.

We are currently some distance from this goal. In 1989, 29 percent of the U.S. population was under age 21, but 36 percent of the uninsured were under 21. Over 12 million children under the age of 21 were uninsured in that year.[1] In 1990, 433,000 pregnant women, or 9 percent, had no health insurance.[2]

Part of the explanation for the high incidence of being uninsured is that many children and pregnant women are not insured directly but are the indirect beneficiaries of a parent's or spouse's employment-based private insurance. Being one step removed from the source of insurance—that is, receiving coverage as a dependent—is an increasingly expensive and insecure basis upon which to receive health care coverage, even assuming the parent or spouse is employed. Because the cost of insurance for dependents is rising, employers are ever more reluctant to meet the full cost of that coverage. In 1980, 40 percent of employers paid

---

1. Foley (1991).
2. National Commission on Children (1991), p. 137.

the full cost of dependent coverage; in 1990, only 33 percent did so.[3] Such trends underlie the finding that 23 percent of uninsured children live in families with insured parents. A report published by the Children's Defense Fund notes that even children in traditional families with two parents and one wage earner were not immune to the decline in private health insurance coverage. Their coverage rate dropped from 83 percent in 1977 to 73 percent in 1987.[4]

Principally to contain costs, health insurance plans may exclude certain groups with special relevance to maternal and child health. These include adolescents and young adults not yet insured on their own who have attained the age of majority, undocumented residents, adopted children, children who are living with their grandparents or an older sibling, and dependent adult children. Over time, all these exclusions should go. Health insurance should be continuously available—regardless of employment status, family income, age, health, marital status, family composition, or geographic location, and regardless of changes in these factors. In particular, a change in the employment status of an adult should not disrupt the health insurance coverage of his or her dependents.

The exclusion of undocumented residents is of special relevance to maternal and child health because many in this group are mothers, children, and pregnant women. Of the 2 million to 4 million undocumented people in the United States at present, most are women. Women of reproductive age (15 to 44) are believed to account for 30 to 40 percent of undocumented residents; 20 percent are believed to be children under 15.[5] Undocumented residents also add significantly to the costs of uncompensated care provided by hospitals in states such as Texas, California, Florida, New York, and Illinois, where there are large populations of such individuals.

Ensuring access to health insurance is the cornerstone of most proposals to improve the U.S. health care system. It is a concept that a wide variety of groups have grasped, and around which coalitions can form and cohere. But the simple availability of health insurance will not assure access to health care for children and mothers. Although having a source of payment for care helps matters greatly, there remain important barriers to care for children and pregnant women.[6] These obstacles include benefit packages that do not reflect the health care needs of this population; inadequate diversity, supply, and distribution of providers; poorly organized or even absent health care services in inner cities and

---

3. National Commission on Children (1991), p. 136.
4. Rosenbaum and others (1992), p. 17, table 4.
5. Passel (1991).
6. Brown (1988).

rural communities; tangled relationships between public and private systems of care; and insufficient collection and evaluation of data to monitor the health of children and pregnant women. Securing a reliable and adequate source of payment for health care, which is the major focus of most current proposals, is clearly a crucial first step, but it is only a first step.

Emphasizing Primary and Preventive Care

Second, health insurance should emphasize primary and preventive care, should include the diagnosis and management of a variety of diseases and conditions, and should include specialized care for complex health problems.

Deciding which services should be financed by health insurance has proven to be one of the most contentious issues in health policy. Especially for maternal and child health, many of the most important services do not fit well with a risk-based insurance model. Many therapeutic interventions are as much educational, social, and behavioral as they are medical.

If resources were unlimited, agreement could probably be reached quickly about the health services that should be available to pregnant women and to children. Some arguments might arise about who should provide a particular service (such as assistance in stopping smoking), or whether a particular intervention is really a health service or a social service (for example, respite care). But a consensus would generally be easy to develop. In the face of limited resources, however, disagreements arise about what is an essential health service, what works (or, in current parlance, has been shown to be "effective"), and what benefits should be provided. As a result, private insurance—and even some public programs—may omit services important to children and pregnant women.

Three services illustrate the special needs of children and pregnant women. In part because routine prenatal care has been shown recently to be cost-effective, and in part because of the Pregnancy Discrimination Act of 1978, prenatal care is now included in most private health insurance plans. This represents major progress. Nonetheless, coverage for other pregnancy-related care can be so thin and incomplete that women with high-risk pregnancies can find that coverage applies only to uneventful pregnancies. In areas where high-risk pregnancies are common, such as inner cities, the deleterious effects of this gap in financing can assume major proportions.

Well-child care is also covered inadequately. Immunizations are frequently excluded, and even when they are covered as part of general well-child supervision, such coverage often ceases after a child's first birthday. The recommended immunization schedule alone extends well into middle childhood, however, and the need for periodic health assessments for children continues.

Even worse is the position occupied by family planning services and contraceptive supplies. These services are often excluded from coverage in private plans and are even left out of many of the reform bills now being considered—a situation I find both outrageous and short-sighted. After all my years of work and advocacy in the area of maternal and child health, I've come to the view that improving family planning services might well be the single most useful strategy we could pursue for improving maternal and child health over the long term. The Allan Guttmacher Institute has estimated that 54 percent of pregnancies in 1982 were not intended at time of conception, and they believe that the percentage has grown. Indeed, the rate of unintended pregnancy at time of conception in the United States is probably among the highest in the developed world. Further, it is well known that unintended pregnancy is linked to late or no prenatal care, which in turn is associated with low birthweight and infant mortality. Every year, 1.3 million pregnancies result in unwanted or mistimed births; 1.6 million pregnancies are terminated by induced abortion; and 400,000 unintended pregnancies are miscarried.[7] Can there be any doubt that family planning in the United States is inadequate? How can discussions of improving the health of mothers and children—and of health care reform generally—so often ignore this whole area?

But it is not just low-cost, recurring, and routine services that require attention. Children with serious illnesses and conditions also require a range of services that insurance often does not cover. Some of these services have historically been provided through various networks of care for expensive or relatively rare diseases and conditions of childhood. Regional systems of perinatal care are perhaps the most widely recognized, but networks of specialized care also exist for cystic fibrosis and other low-prevalence disabling conditions and for pediatric emergency services. In any reform of the health care system, the usefulness, function, and future of these networks should be considered, and their valuable components should be given adequate support.

---

7. Klerman (1991).

Offering Health Care
in Nontraditional Settings

Third, we need greater support for offering health services in a wide variety of settings that are effective in reaching children and pregnant women, especially the medically underserved.

Several settings that are well suited for providing care to children and pregnant women are not routinely supported by private third-party payers, and grants to establish and maintain them are often inadequate and unreliable. For example, school-based health clinics, birthing centers, comprehensive community health centers, and home-based health care for certain diseases and conditions have proven both economical and effective, yet have limited support.[8] And now there are proposals to provide comprehensive health care services to children and families in an even wider variety of nontraditional settings, such as preschool and family-support programs.

Extensive experience over the last two decades has demonstrated that meeting the health needs of high-risk pregnant women and children, particularly the very poor, is often accomplished best through a mix of intensive medical and social services provided at a single site.[9] Despite the proven value of such comprehensive centers for high-risk families, they have never had a secure base of funding, and their numbers have always been limited. For example, although about 550 community health centers and mental health centers are currently in operation, only 6 million of the 32 million Americans who are medically underserved receive care through these systems.[10]

We need to provide stable financing for these sites as well as specific services, particularly for those groups often left out of conventional health care arrangements. Putting a Medicaid or an Americare or a Health Plus card in everyone's hand will not be sufficient. We need to support comprehensive care centers, where the services available are broadly conceived and kindly offered.

Increasing the Number
and Diversity of Providers

Fourth, closely related to the issues just covered is the need to increase the number and diversity of providers caring for children and

---

8. Lear and others (1991); Rooks and others (1989); Strobino and others (1986); U.S. Congress, Office of Technology Assessment (1987).

9. Brown (1988), pp. 64–65.

10. National Commission on Children (1991), p. 149.

pregnant women. At present, there are not enough well-trained, licensed providers to care for children and pregnant women who have low incomes, are at high risk medically, or live in inner cities or rural areas. For example, over the last several years, the number of obstetricians serving these groups and these areas has declined, as has the number of family physicians practicing obstetrics; the latter provide over two-thirds of the obstetrical care in rural areas.[11] Similarly, a slight decline in the number of pediatricians who take Medicaid patients has also been noted recently.[12] Simply put, the geographical distribution of providers does not match the need for services, and in some instances there are simply too few providers.

The problem of provider maldistribution is exceedingly complicated and reflects longstanding patterns of practice and payment. Although a single reform plan may not be able to solve this problem quickly and efficiently, it should nonetheless take some constructive steps. One time-tested method of addressing the problem is to fund special clinics in underserved areas, as described directly above. Five other solutions have merit: (1) placing health care providers in medically underserved areas through the National Health Service Corps and similar programs; (2) using more mid-level practitioners in appropriate settings; (3) improving the medical liability situation; (4) encouraging private providers to accept more patients whose care is paid for by public funds; and (5) increasing the emphasis in graduate medical education on primary and community-based care.

Of all these, my favorite is expanding the use of certified nurse-midwives, obstetric and gynecologic nurse-practitioners, and similar mid-level personnel in the health care system. Certified nurse-midwives, for example, have been shown repeatedly to be especially well suited to providing many of the preventive and primary care services needed by pregnant women, and they have a long tradition of serving in low-income and rural communities.[13] Nonetheless, the use of midwives is constrained by the limited number of training opportunities, the unstable availability of malpractice insurance, the continuing reluctance of some physicians to collaborate with nonphysicians, and the refusal of some insurers to reimburse for health services provided by such practitioners. A proposal to reform the health care system should support the use of mid-level practitioners in organized settings (such as community health centers and hospital clinics) and in collaborative arrangements with physicians, make certain that adequate numbers of training slots are

---

11. Weiner and Engel (1991).
12. Yudkowsky, Cartland, and Flint (1990).
13. Rooks and Haas (1986).

available, ensure access of practitioners to malpractice insurance, and require adequate reimbursement for their services.

Preserving Public Health Programs

Fifth, we must assess and, where appropriate, preserve in some form the government grant programs that now finance health services for children and pregnant women, along with health planning, evaluation, and training.

Expanding the availability and affordability of health insurance intensifies the ongoing debate about the future role and structure of the public health system in providing personal health services, and it raises specific questions about the fate of many public health grant programs. Programs that are especially important to children and pregnant women include the following:

- The maternal and child health services block grant
- The preventive health services block grant
- Grants to states for childhood immunization
- Pediatric emergency medical services
- Title X family planning services
- The demonstration program in care for children with AIDS
- Grants for injury control
- Grants for prevention and abatement of lead poisoning
- Poison control activities.

Many of these programs provide health services to those with no source of payment for health care, and some are providers of last resort. Some serve special populations or provide important health services that third-party reimbursement does not cover. A 1988 report estimated that programs supported by the maternal and child health block grant provided over one-half million women with prenatal care, accounting for almost 14 percent of all babies born and well over one-third of births to low-income women; they also provided basic well-child health services to over 2 1/2 million infants, children, and youths.[14]

The importance of these public health grants demands that their role be considered carefully when reforming the health care system. Are they to be eliminated? Folded into a new public system? Retained as is? If the intent is to fund all, or most, personal health services through insurance, what is to be the fate of the other functions that public health grants often support—planning, needs assessment, data collection and

---

14. Association of Maternal and Child Health Programs (1991).

analysis, training, and the like? Answers to these questions are vital to the future of the public health system, of which maternal and child health services are only a part.

Designing Managed Care Arrangements

Sixth, cost management measures must accommodate the special needs of children and pregnant women.

With the relentless escalation of health care costs, cost containment has become a major force behind health care reform. Any reform proposal must include specific measures for keeping national health expenditures at some reasonable, acceptable proportion of national income. Containing the growth of health costs is vital to preserving scarce national resources for competing needs.

One popular cost management approach is managed care. This art form deserves special comment because of its growing popularity as a tool for limiting costs for the privately insured as well as for children and pregnant women insured by Medicaid. Managed care systems have developed largely in response to various problems in the fee-for-service system, including the steady rise in health care costs. These new arrangements attempt to contain costs by negotiating reduced fees with providers enrolled in the system, limiting consumers' freedom of choice, and, in theory, improving the care of patients through a broadening of access to private physicians (in the case of Medicaid) and an increase in monitoring of provider behavior. Despite their growing popularity, however, managed care systems have yet to demonstrate conclusively that they contain costs.

The critical issue here is whether managed care meets the health care needs of mothers and children. Limited data and anecdotal experience with managed care for children and pregnant women raise several concerns.[15] First, because inappropriate or excessive hospitalizations and referrals to specialists occur proportionately more for adults than for children, there may be little need in a pediatric population for the gatekeeper function that managed care offers. Second, managed care networks may place strict limits on access to providers who are not enrolled in the plan, even when providers who are in the plan lack the needed skills or have skills of lower quality. Although such limits may be appropriate for essentially well children, they can pose major obstacles to necessary, appropriate care for children with more serious or rare diseases and conditions. Third, managed care can generate conflicts between providing good medical care and containing costs. For example, a

15. Behrman (1991).

growing number of managed care plans deny more than 24 hours of hospitalization after a normal vaginal delivery and limit coverage of postpartum home-based nursing care for patients discharged that early.

If a reform proposal incorporates managed care, it should not only contain costs but also provide for high-quality, appropriate care. Thus the proposal should specify that managed care will be evaluated not only on limiting costs but also on ensuring access to needed services and achieving better health.

The fee-for-service system, however, has drawbacks beyond its role in the inflation of health care costs. For example, it is associated with the overuse of physician services, tests, and procedures and affords only poor coordination among individual providers. Thus all forms of medical practice—fee-for-service, managed care, and other arrangements—require careful oversight for both cost and quality.

Achieving Administrative Simplicity

The seventh and final issue is the importance of administrative simplicity in the health care system, both for the families who use it and for the providers who work in it. Private insurance is often difficult to comprehend; Medicaid can be even worse. Providers report that the intricacy and cumbersome procedures of some insurance plans, and of Medicaid in particular, discourage their participation. Clearly, frustration with the complexity of the current U.S. health care system is one of the strongest forces pushing the reform debate.[16] This is a problem for everyone, but particularly for children and pregnant women. Children must depend on adults to arrange for their health care, and pregnancy is a ticking clock, requiring concentrated care in a relatively brief time. In both cases, care delayed by administrative complexity is care denied.

A reform plan should therefore simplify procedures for enrollment, participation, and payment, particularly in multipayer systems. If we continue with the patchwork system of thousands of private plans, over fifty Medicaid plans, high-risk pools for the "medically uninsurable," and numerous other public plans, then we must figure out how people can move between financing systems without losing coverage and without suffering a nervous breakdown due to paperwork.

---

16. Himmelstein and Woolhandler (1986).

Conclusion

To summarize, ensuring access to health insurance for all will not be enough, especially for children and pregnant women, because access to health insurance is not the same as access to health care. Any reform of the American health care system should emphasize primary and preventive care for children and pregnant women, provide health care for them in appropriate settings, increase the number and diversity of providers, preserve needed public health function, design managed care arrangements to accommodate the special needs of mothers and children, and guarantee administrative simplicity.

Clearly, those who know the problems of children as they relate to this complicated area of social policy have not yet made their presence felt. But it is not too late to bring these issues to light.

References

Association of Maternal and Child Health Programs. *Making a Difference: A Report on Title V Maternal and Child Health Services Programs' Role in Reducing Infant Mortality.* Washington: The Association, 1991.

Behrman, Richard E. Personal communication. David and Lucile Packard Foundation, Los Altos, CA, August 1991.

Brown, Sarah S., editor. *Prenatal Care: Reaching Mothers, Reaching Infants.* Washington: Institute of Medicine, National Academy Press, 1988.

Foley, Jill. *Uninsured in the United States: The Nonelderly Population without Health Insurance—Analysis of the March 1990 Current Population Survey.* Special Report SR-10. Employee Benefit Research Institute, Washington, April 1991.

Himmelstein, David U., and Steffie Woolhandler. "Cost Without Benefit: Administrative Waste in U.S. Health Care," *New England Journal of Medicine,* vol. 314 (1986), pp. 441–45.

Klerman, L.V. Personal communication. Washington, 1991.

Lear, Julia Graham, and others. "Reorganizing Health Care for Adolescents: The Experience of the School-Based Adolescent Health Care Program," *Journal of Adolescent Health,* vol. 12 (1991), pp. 450–58.

National Commission on Children. *Beyond Rhetoric: A New American Agenda for Children and Families.* Washington: The Commission, 1991.

Passel, Jeffrey. Personal communication. Urban Institute, Washington, December 1991.

Peoples, Mary Dennis, and others. "Evaluation of the Effects of the North Carolina Improved Pregnancy Outcome Project: Implications for

State-Level Decision-Making," *American Journal of Public Health*, vol. 74 (1984), pp. 549–54.

Rooks, Judith P., and Eugene J. Haas, editors. *Nurse-Midwifery in America*. Washington: American College of Nurse-Midwives Foundation, 1986.

_____, and others. "Outcomes of Care in Birth Centers: The National Birth Center Study," *New England Journal of Medicine*, vol. 321 (1989), pp. 1804–11.

Rosenbaum, Sara, and others. "Children and Health Insurance." Washington: Children's Defense Fund, 1992.

Strobino, Donna M., and others. "The Impact of the Mississippi Improved Child Health Project on Prenatal Care and Low Birthweight," *American Journal of Public Health*, vol. 76 (1986), pp. 274–78.

U.S. Congress, Office of Technology Assessment. *Technology-Dependent Children: Hospital vs. Home Care*. Philadelphia: J.B. Lippincott, 1987.

Weiner, Joshua M., and Jeannie Engel. *Improving Access to Health Services for Children and Pregnant Women*. Washington: Brookings Institution, 1991.

Yudkowsky, B.K., J.D.C. Cartland, and S.S. Flint. "Pediatric Participation in Medicaid: 1978 to 1989," *Pediatrics*, vol. 85 (1990), pp. 567–77.

COMMENTS

Lawrence D. Brown

Sarah Brown's paper lays out the issues in children's health succinctly and convincingly. In my comments, I want to focus on three questions: Why is children's health a timely issue? Why is children's health not a higher priority? What can be done to move children's health forward on the political agenda?

Why Is Children's Health a Timely Issue?

The main point of Sarah Brown's paper is that reforming the health insurance system is not the same thing as reforming the health care system. As she says, access to health insurance does not assume access to health care. That difference matters a lot for children, especially for poor children.

Children's health is a timely issue because, I think, we are on the verge of a reform of the health care system that may eventually lead to universal coverage. That 35 million people are uninsured has not spurred action. That the middle class must now worry about the affordability of health coverage has turned health care into a mainstream issue. As a result, significant reform of the health care system seems to be imminent at last.

Lawrence D. Brown is a professor and head of the Division of Health Policy and Management in the School of Public Health at Columbia University.

If health insurance coverage is to be universal and affordable, the budgetary and regulatory roles of the federal government must expand dramatically. I doubt that meaningful reform in the health insurance market for small groups can take place without significant public subsidies, and I doubt that the states will be willing or able to provide those subsidies. Tax credits for health insurance may be financed in part by capping Medicaid or Medicare but ultimately will require additional federal dollars. A play-or-pay plan will require businesses to pick up some of the costs of health insurance but will still require a new public program as a backup. If so, major reform of the insurance industry is likely to follow because the federal government will not permit private insurers to shift all the bad risks to the public sector. The federal government will also get tougher with providers on cost containment issues. And the federal and state governments will struggle over the allocation of costs.

I foresee a protracted conflict among federal reformers, the insurance industry, the business community, health care providers, and the states. The issues will not be resolved easily, and clashes will continue for years. The conflict will center on the redefinition of the risk-based insurance system, and in the process, as Sarah Brown rightly points out, the public health system may be largely ignored. What should be done about block grants for preventive health services, childhood immunization programs, efforts to prevent lead poisoning, community health centers, mental health centers, and the other programs that Sarah Brown discussed? They may well get lost in the shuffle.

Why Is Children's Health
Not a Higher Priority?

Second, why are children not so influential a political force as one might think? Of course, they do not vote. They do not send their allowances to political action committees. They do not employ millions of people, unlike the health insurance industry. They are not highly paid scientific professionals.

But people have considerable sympathy for children. The cost of their health care is not all that high, as we keep pointing out. Moreover, if we fail to invest in the health of our children, they will not grow up to be productive workers who can compete with the Japanese.

And so we have a political paradox. Children are an attractive political cause, yet their needs are poorly served. One reason is that such large sums go to the uncontrollable entitlement programs, especially Medicare and Medicaid, that little remains for children. Another is that people believe that children are generally healthy, so that there is no real problem.

The most important reason, however, may be that our concerns about children are so many and so diverse that they cannot be encompassed by a single policy. Instead, our policy is diffuse and fragmented and involves many different programs. It includes prenatal care for mothers, treatment of medically handicapped newborns, well-child and preventive care, immunizations, family planning, and mental health. It also comprises prevention of substance abuse, child abuse, suicide, and homicide. Formulating children's health policy involves many different constituencies, bureaucracies, funding sources, technologies of service delivery, legislative committees, and advocates with diverse priorities.

Setting policy for the elderly is far more centripetal, involving mainly Social Security and Medicare. Long-term care is more diffuse, but even that debate is more circumscribed than those surrounding child health policy.

Child health groups compete for the attention of specialized policymakers and legislators. They also compete for what little money is left after the entitlements have consumed their share. Although in making child health policy, we always aim for comprehensiveness, continuity, and integration, the reality often involves fragmentation and competition. In facing the coming political storm over health insurance reform, however, unity and coherence will be all the more important.

What Can Be Done?

What can we do to get more attention for children's health? How do we make the case for these small programs that are so vital to children, especially disadvantaged children? I have three suggestions.

First, keep pressing the point that health insurance reform while necessary is not sufficient. For poor children—for children in general—the adequacy of health services depends on the appropriateness of the structure for service delivery. This means a mix of generalist, multiservice agencies and specialized regional networks. Caught up in the details of reimbursement formulas and the like, policymakers often find this point elusive. Many legislators view such items as mere details of implementation, to be taken up after everything else has been settled.

Second, when budgetary pressures are tight, the program with a convincing, documented claim to cost-effectiveness stands out from the crowd of claimants. This argument is one of the resources that has enabled Representative Henry Waxman and his colleagues to expand Medicaid at regular intervals. But the case must be made over and over, program by program. Fortunately, many health services researchers will be more than delighted to help you make such a case.

Third, we should remember that every nation with universal health insurance coverage has better child health programs than we do. We ought to look more closely at how they finance these services and, equally important, how they integrate their health care delivery and financing systems. It must be doable; every other comparable nation is doing it.

COMMENTS

Charles N. Kahn, III

I agree with Sarah Brown's analysis. Her paper makes some convincing arguments why play-or-pay is no answer to many of the questions that are being raised about health care. I want to focus on two problem areas—the poor quality of the political debate and the avoidance of redistributional issues.

The Nature of the Political Debate

Like everyone else at this conference, I am excited that health care has finally made it into prime time. Health is now number two on the hit parade of popular issues, ranking just below the economy. But this new discussion of health seems unlikely to produce any wisdom.

I am afraid that the issue of health will be Willy Hortonized over the next few months. I see the political debate splitting into two parts, neither of which is going to address the critical issues or details that have been considered at this conference.

On one side, President Bush is talking about reform largely in terms of bottom-up cost containment—getting people at the grass roots to figure out how to solve the cost problem. In some ways, the President is attributing much of the problem to overconsumption and growth in the volume and intensity of services.

Charles N. Kahn, III, is minority health counsel to the House Committee on Ways and Means.

On the other side, Democrats are for universal coverage and top-down cost containment. They blame the providers and the insurers for overcharging and doing things they shouldn't be doing.

If President Bush wins reelection, you will see incremental reform. If the Democrats win, you will see play-or-pay or some other kind of national health insurance. And if the Congress does try to enact play-or-pay, the outcome will be a mess, partly because it will try to do it on the cheap. Then, as Larry Brown predicts, we will need all kinds of mid-course corrections, and we may come to rue the day that a true national health policy was put in place.

Redistributional Issues

Why aren't children front and center in discussions of health policy? The reason is that it is concern for the insured—not the uninsured—that has made health an important issue. The American people are less concerned about fairness and equity than about their own health care and their own health insurance. For example, if you have health insurance, you are angry because your coinsurance and deductibles have gone up and you must pay more out of your own pocket. If the business you are working for is sputtering, then you worry about your coverage. If you have a dependent, or if you have a chronic illness, you wonder whether you can find a job you like with the coverage you need.

For the middle class, most of the health care issues we are considering here are not pressing. Middle-class children are generally healthy, and their parents make enough money to pay for their shots, treatment of ear infections, and other necessary care.

Many of the children's issues considered here relate to socioeconomic factors, and those are not the issues that have put health on prime time. Members of Congress worry much more about the issues that are bothering the middle class. Also, the lesson of Medicare catastrophic coverage has not been lost on them.

The point is this: Americans are not very enthusiastic about redistribution, particularly when they think it may adversely affect them. We can say that the arguments against Medicare catastrophic health insurance and its funding mechanism were unfair, that it was really only a small group of people who would have paid a lot more money to fund the enhanced benefits for others. But perceptions are everything. If the middle class believes that they will be made worse off by a reform that is supposedly helping them, there will be trouble in River City.

COMMENTS

Sara Rosenbaum

I want to reflect on the last fifteen years of change in maternal and child health to see whether they have taught us any lessons from the past and given us any hope for the future.

What Has Been Done

My involvement with national policy on maternal and child health dates from 1976, when I became involved in the Child Health Assurance Act (CHAP) legislation. That bill was the first attempt since the inception of Medicaid to restructure the program to reach more poor children.

From the time we started working on CHAP, it took eight years to establish in law the proposition that if a child lived at 20 percent of the federal poverty level but had two parents at home, the child should still have Medicaid.

It took ten years for states to be given the option to extend Medicaid coverage to all poor children up to the age of five and to pregnant women.

It took twelve years to accept the idea that all pregnant women and all infants eligible for subsidized food under WIC also should have Medicaid coverage.

Sara Rosenbaum is a senior fellow at George Washington University's Center for Health Policy Research and a senior attorney at the Children's Defense Fund.

It took thirteen years to establish the principle that a poor two-year-old who needs physical therapy for a developmental disability should get that therapy no matter what state the baby lives in.

It took about thirteen years to improve Medicaid payment rates for primary health care services in medically underserved areas, with the aim of promoting their development.

It took fourteen years to change federal Medicaid law so that a child or pregnant woman can apply for benefits at a health clinic.

It will take until 2002, at the current rate, to assure that all poor children under 19 have Medicaid coverage, because we are phasing in the coverage for them on a year-by-year basis. In a country with a $1.5 trillion budget, we couldn't find the money to cover all poor children at once.

In a nutshell, it will have taken a total of twenty-six years, starting in 1976, to add all poor children and pregnant women to the Medicaid population.

Further Incremental Changes

Here are some of the things that child health advocates want to get done.

We want every disabled child who is eligible for supplemental security income (SSI) to have a Medicaid card. In some states, children on SSI still cannot receive Medicaid.

We want Medicaid enrollment to last a year at a time so that children have some hope of establishing an enduring relationship with a provider of health care.

We want Medicaid coverage that travels with migrant children so that children whose families have to move around to work can carry their insurance with them.

We want a few hundred more community health centers and migrant health centers in underserved areas.

We want enough obstetricians, pediatricians, and dentists to staff the health centers already in operation.

We want families to be able to get Medicaid for their children even if the value of their automobiles is $1,800 and not $1,500.

We want uninsured children to be eligible for Medicaid even if their family's income is 110 percent of poverty and not 100 percent of poverty.

And we certainly want to establish the right of all children to free vaccinations. It now costs $125 to vaccinate a 15-month-old. Many American families cannot easily bear this expense.

This list of incremental changes may suggest that I think we will be lucky just to get Medicaid working for poor children better than it works today. But if all we have to show for our efforts by the end of the decade is a better Medicaid program, we will not have done our job.

Moving toward Comprehensive Reform

Medicaid was the focus of reform in the 1980s because it was the only available vehicle. Nobody was prepared to talk about anything broader than improvements in Medicaid. Many of us who were involved in the effort to reform Medicaid believed that it was the only way to focus policy on issues that people were not otherwise ready to debate. For example, establishing the proposition that a child's Medicaid coverage should be a separate issue from her need for food stamps or welfare benefits or from the family's living arrangements took a long time. The only place we had to make the case for equity in insurance coverage was the Medicaid program.

The changes in Medicaid reflect important changes in the public perception of insurance. They have also created a financial base on which to build. In the world of budgeting, the current services baseline for federal child health expenditures is vastly higher than it was a decade ago. The next leap in child health is now financially possible.

Two things will promote further progress over the next decade. First, many people have come to see the fundamental problems with incremental changes in health care. Piecemeal changes in Medicaid that should have happened all at once have been burdensome for federal and state agencies to administer. They have also led to constantly evolving financial eligibility rules, categorical eligibility rules, and enrollment procedures, as well as different levels of federal financial support for various services and providers. It would have been much better to make all the changes at once and then leave this complex program alone for a number of years.

The second factor that will help us make a bigger leap is the very fact that the problems of children's insurance and child health have become so widespread. At the rate we are going, by the end of the decade 50 percent of white children and 80 percent of black children will not have employer-based health insurance. More and more families are feeling the pinch. Primary health care for children now costs several hundred dollars per year, a not insignificant amount for millions of families. Over the coming years, so many families will be hurting that policymakers will have to radically restructure Medicaid or integrate it into a much broader program.

The conceptual groundwork has been laid. The financial groundwork has been laid. In the next decade, if we persist, we can get where we need to go.

COMMENTS

Bruce C. Vladeck

Sarah Brown's main point is that insurance coverage is a necessary but not sufficient condition for getting poor children the health care services they need. How, then, as we move in the direction of universal health insurance, do we go about providing health services for children? And what additional services should we provide for particularly disadvantaged children that health insurance would not ordinarily cover?

I will comment on these questions based on my experience in helping to provide health care to children in New York City. But I am sure that the problems are much the same for poor children in Anacostia, on the south side of Chicago, in east Los Angeles, and in hundreds of other places around the country.

Health Care as Part of a Larger Problem

It is clear to me that we have, in our inner cities, a complicated set of social problems interacting with and reinforcing one another. We have a generation of children who come from low-income families and, disproportionately, from single-parent households. The health care system fails these children. The public educational system is a disgrace. And, in my part of the country at least, the child welfare system has totally collapsed.

Bruce C. Vladeck is president of the United Hospital Fund of New York.

In New York City, some 60,000 children are under the aegis of what was formerly called the child welfare system. But the system that is supposed to ensure the well-being of those children has lost almost all its capacity to protect them and to provide them with the necessary social services. In the 1980s, as states paid for the inflation of Medicaid costs, they gutted the staff and the operational capacities of the human service and social service agencies, particularly in large cities and particularly those that served children most in need of medical care.

Our capacity to intervene in situations of domestic violence, for example, has just about disappeared. One statistic from New York is, I think, reflective of what goes on throughout the country. Of the 60,000 children who were, at one time or another during 1990, under the jurisdiction of the family court and the child protective system in New York City, ninety died. Twenty-four of these deaths were homicides.

Many of the failures that cause children to need health care are in what we traditionally think of as the educational system, the social service system, the child protection system, or the criminal justice system, which touches the lives of more adolescents in the City of New York than the health care system does. But it is a sad fact that as a society we are more willing to pay for medical care for poor children than we are to provide income support, social services, early childhood education, or other more cost-effective services. Until we deal with the basic issues of income, education, class, and culture in poor communities, we will merely be applying Band Aids. By not reducing the incidence of violence, for example, we will pay more for the doctors who deal with trauma in emergency rooms.

Special Needs of Adolescents

The United Hospital Fund and I have become particularly concerned about issues relating to the health care of adolescents. Although we generally think of adolescents as being very healthy, they constitute the group most at risk of infection by HIV and other sexually transmitted diseases. Soon, we will be talking about an epidemic of drug-resistant tuberculosis among teenagers in New York City. And, for a whole variety of reasons, it is extremely hard to reach adolescents with health care services.

We talk a lot in New York about problems of cross-cultural service delivery, about the increasing number of clients in the health care system who don't speak English, about having staff who speak Spanish, Creole, Vietnamese, and Russian. But the cultural gap between white, middle-class health care providers and African Americans or Hispanics of the same age is nothing compared to the cultural chasm between the average adult and the average teenager. Again, we must think about comprehensive service strategies and recognize that health insurance is an essential but only an elementary part of the solution.

The Issue of Race

These observations lead to my last point, which I believe is critical. Most of the adolescents with whom we have been working in New York City, and many of the beneficiaries of social welfare programs, are children of color.

As a culture and as a society, we hate teenagers. More important, in big cities, including New York and Washington and those where a majority of our minority teenagers live, we not only hate teenagers in general; we particularly hate black and Hispanic teenagers. We are afraid of them, and we attribute to them most of the deterioration of the communities in which we live. That is the cultural and psychological background for designing and financing social service systems.

Chip Kahn described health care as an issue that pits the middle class against deprived groups in the population. His analysis was correct, in my view, but it doesn't go far enough. We still don't talk bluntly enough in this society about race. The fact is that the children in the inner cities about whose problems I have been talking are predominantly minority children.

For a long time, advocates for the poor have found an unemployed white person, preferably an eastern European ethnic construction worker, to be our model. And we always emphasized the high proportion of AFDC recipients who are white.

Increasingly, however, the crisis in health care, the lack of health insurance, and the high mortality and morbidity are most glaring in the ghettoes of our inner cities. And the children in these ghettoes are more heavily minority than is the rest of the population.

The racial and ethnic composition of the population of children is different from that of the voting population. It contains considerably more African Americans and Hispanics than the adult population does, as school tax referendums all over the country keep demonstrating.

We advocates must recognize that the gap between our words and actions emerges not only from budgetary constraints, an anti-governmental climate, and political ideology, but also from a critical racial component. In this sense, health care has already become Willy Hortonized. Unless we face up to this development, we will not succeed in getting the services our children need.

ABOUT THE PRESENTERS

MARY JO BANE became commissioner of the New York State Department of Public Welfare on April 6, 1992. Dr. Bane, who served as executive deputy commissioner of the department from 1984 to 1986, had been the director of the Malcolm Wiener Center for Social Policy at the Kennedy School of Government, Harvard University. From 1980 to 1981, she served as deputy assistant secretary for planning and budget in the U.S. Department of Education. Dr. Bane is the author of numerous books and articles on human services and public policy, including *The State and the Poor in the 1980s* and *Here to Stay: American Families in the Twentieth Century*. She received a doctorate in education and a master of arts in teaching from Harvard University.

DOUGLAS J. BESHAROV is a lawyer and a resident scholar at the American Enterprise Institute for Public Policy Research in Washington, D.C.. He also is a professor of family law and policy at Georgetown University. Mr. Besharov's most recent book is *Recognizing Child Abuse: A Guide for the Concerned*, which is designed to help professionals and laypersons identify and report suspected child abuse. He has written or edited thirteen other books, including *Legal Services for the Poor: Time for Reform* and *The Vulnerable Social Worker: Liability for Serving Children and Families*. Mr. Besharov received his J.D. from New York University.

LAWRENCE D. BROWN is a professor and the head of the Division of Health Policy and Management in the School of Public Health at Columbia University. He was previously on the faculty of the University of Michigan and the staff of the Brookings Institution. Professor Brown writes on competitive and regulatory issues in health policy and on the politics of health care policymaking more generally. He has evaluated (with Catherine McLaughlin) the Robert Wood Johnson Foundation's community programs for affordable health care and its health program for the uninsured. He was editor of the *Journal of Health Politics, Policy and Law*. Professor Brown received his doctorate in government from Harvard University.

SARAH S. BROWN is senior study director for the National Forum on the Future of Children and Families, which is a joint project of the Institute of Medicine and the National Research Council. From 1986 to 1989, Ms. Brown was the study director of the Prenatal Care Outreach Program for the Institute of Medicine. Ms. Brown is the author of several publications, including *A Pound of Prevention: The Case for Universal Access to Maternity Care*, and editor of *Children and Parental Illicit Drug Use: Research, Clinical, and Policy Issues, Preventing Low Birthweight, Prenatal Care,* and *Including Children and Pregnant Women in Health Care Reform*. She received her M.S. in public health from the University of North Carolina.

ALLAN C. CARLSON has been the president of the Rockford Institute in Illinois since 1986. In 1988, he was appointed by President Reagan to the National Commission on Children, on which he served through 1991. Mr. Carlson has written extensively on the subjects of modern social history, family policy, the relationship between foreign and domestic policies, the interaction of economics and culture, and modern religion. His books include *Family Questions: Reflections on the American Social Crises* and *The Swedish Experiment in Family Politics: The Myrdals and the Interwar Population Crises*. He received his doctorate in modern European history from Ohio University.

IRWIN GARFINKEL is currently a professor of social work at Columbia University. Previously, he was the Edwin E. Witte Professor of Social Work and director of the Institute for Research on Poverty at the University of Wisconsin. His principal teaching and research interest is social welfare policy, particularly income transfer programs. Mr. Garfinkel is the author of several books, including *Income Tested Transfer Programs: The Case For and Against, Single Mothers and Their Children: A New American Dilemma?*, and *Assuring Child Support: An Extension of Social Security*. Mr. Garfinkel received his doctorate in social work and economics from the University of Michigan.

OLIVIA GOLDEN is director of programs and policy at the Children's Defense Fund. From 1987 to 1991, she was a lecturer in public policy at the John F. Kennedy School of Government at Harvard University. She is the author of the forthcoming book, *Poor Children and Welfare Reform*. Ms. Golden has been involved in numerous community activities, including the Cambridge Advisory Committee on Children and Youth, the Mental Health Board for the Cambridge–Somerville Area, and the Massachusetts State Democratic Convention. She received her doctorate in public policy from Harvard University.

ROBERT GREENSTEIN is the founder and executive director of the Center on Budget and Policy Priorities, a nonprofit organization established to analyze federal and state budget and policy issues that affect low- and moderate-income Americans. He is a policy analyst on a range of low-income programs and poverty issues. Previously, Mr. Greenstein was director of the Project on Food Assistance and Poverty, and administrator of the Food and Nutrition Service at the U.S. Department of Agriculture. Mr. Greenstein received his A.B. from Harvard College and has done graduate work at the University of California-Berkeley.

JUDITH M. GUERON is president of the Manpower Demonstration Research Corporation. She is currently leading MDRC's eight-year effort to evaluate a new national welfare reform program, the Job Opportunities and Basic Skills Training Program, under a contract with the U.S. Department of Health and Human Services. Dr. Gueron is coauthor of *From Welfare to Work* (Russell Sage Foundation, 1991). She has written extensively on the results of MDRC's demonstrations and the effects of public programs designed to improve the prospects of disadvantaged people, and has served on a number of advisory panels to the U.S. Department of Labor and the National Academy of Sciences. She was awarded the 1988 Myrdal Prize for Evaluation Practice from the American Evaluation Association. She received her doctorate in economics from Harvard University.

DAVID A. HAMBURG, M.D., has been president of the Carnegie Corporation of New York since 1983. From 1984 to 1986, he served as president, then chairman of the board, of the American Association for the Advancement of Science. From 1975 to 1980, he was president of the Institute of Medicine, National Academy of Sciences. He also was the director of the Division of Health Policy Research and Education and John D. MacArthur Professor of Health Policy at Harvard University. Dr. Hamburg is a trustee of Stanford University, the Rockefeller University, the Mount Sinai Medical Center, the American Museum of Natural History, and the Johann Jacobs Foundation. He is the chairman of the Carnegie Council on Adolescent Development and founder of the Carnegie Commission on Science, Technology and Government. Dr. Hamburg received his M.D. from Indiana University.

CHARLES N. (CHIP) KAHN, III, is the minority health counsel to the House Committee on Ways and Means. From 1984 to 1986, he was senior health policy advisor to Senator Dave Durenberger (R-MN), then chairman of the Subcommittee on Health of the Senate Finance Committee. Mr. Kahn also served as legislative assistant for health to Senator Dan Quayle (R-IN) from 1983 to 1984. From 1980 to 1983, he served as director of the Office of Financial Management Education at the Association of University Programs in Health Administration. Before going to AUPHA, Mr. Kahn completed an administrative residency with the teaching hospital department of the Association of American Medical Colleges. He teaches at George Washington University and Tulane University. Mr. Kahn received his M.P.H. from the Tulane University School of Public Health and Tropical Medicine.

GWENDOLYN S. KING was Commissioner of Social Security from 1989 to 1992. She administered the nation's Social Security programs—old-age, survivors, and disability insurance—as well as the means-tested supplemental security income program for elderly, blind, and disabled persons. Previously, Mrs. King was the executive vice president of the Washington firm of Gogol and Associates. From 1986 to 1988, Mrs. King served as deputy assistant to the President and director of the Office of Intergovernmental Affairs at the White House. She has received numerous awards, including the 1990 Drum Major for Justice Award from the Southern Christian Leadership Conference, the 1990 Special Recognition Award of the Denver Urban League, and the 1991 Howard University Alumni Award for Postgraduate Achievement. Mrs. King received her M.S. in public service from the University of Maryland.

LAWRENCE M. MEAD is an associate professor of politics at New York University. In 1987 Professor Mead was Visiting Distinguished Professor at the Institute of Public Affairs, University of Wisconsin-Madison. He is the author of *Beyond Entitlement,* an argument for work requirements in welfare, and *The New Politics of Poverty,* a study of the effects of poverty on American politics. Professor Mead received his doctorate in political science from Harvard University.

RUDOLPH G. PENNER is director of economic studies at KPMG Peat Marwick. He was formerly a senior fellow at the Urban Institute. From 1983 to 1987, Mr. Penner was the director of the Congressional Budget Office. He also served as the director of fiscal policy studies and was a resident scholar at the American Enterprise Institute for Public Policy Research. He is the past president of the National Association of Business Economists. In 1989, he was elected to the board of directors of

NABE, and received the Abraham Prize for the best article published in 1988–89 in *Business Economics*. His most recent book is *Broken Purse Strings*, a study of the congressional budget process written with Alan J. Abramson. In addition, he recently edited *The Great Fiscal Experiment*. Mr. Penner received his Ph.D. in economics from Johns Hopkins University.

WENDELL E. PRIMUS is the chief economist for the House Committee on Ways and Means and staff director of its Subcommittee on Human Resources. In this capacity, he is responsible for budget-related analysis, and he was deeply involved in drafting the Gramm–Rudman–Hollings law. He is also the editor of the Committee's annual *Green Book*. Previously, he was an assistant professor of economics at Georgetown University and a part-time consultant to the House Committee on Agriculture on the food stamp program. Mr. Primus received his Ph.D. in economics from Iowa State University.

SARA ROSENBAUM is a senior fellow at George Washington University's Center for Health Policy Research. Ms. Rosenbaum is also a senior attorney at the Children's Defense Fund, an adjunct professor at Georgetown University's Law Center, and an adjunct assistant professor at the Johns Hopkins University School of Public Health. She has been the director of both programs and policy and the health division of the Children's Defense Fund. She is the author of several publications, including *On the Edge: Children and Health Insurance,* and *The Health of America's Children*. Ms. Rosenbaum received her J.D. from the Boston University School of Law.

LISBETH B. SCHORR is director of the Harvard Project on Effective Services. She has been a lecturer in social medicine at Harvard University since 1984 and is a member of the National Academy of Sciences' Forum on Children and Families. Ms. Schorr chaired the congressionally mandated Select Panel for the Promotion of Child Health between 1978 and 1980, and in the early 1970s helped to establish the health division of the Children's Defense Fund. She was the first lay member of the American Board of Pediatrics, and is a member of the Institute of Medicine of the National Academy of Sciences. Her book, *Within Our Reach: Breaking the Cycle of Disadvantage,* which analyzes the common elements of successful intervention programs, has won several awards. She received her B.A. with highest honors from the University of California.

ISAAC SHAPIRO is a senior research analyst at the Center on Budget and Policy Priorities. Earlier, he was a research associate at the Center for Social Policy Studies. He also has worked as a legislative assistant to Representative Marcy Kaptur (D-Ohio). Mr. Shapiro is the author or coauthor of numerous articles and books, including "Selective Prosperity: Increasing Income Disparities Since 1977," "Far from Fixed: An Analysis of the Unemployment Insurance System," and *Working But Poor: America's Contradiction*. He received his M.S. in public policy from the John F. Kennedy School of Government at Harvard University.

MARGARET C. SIMMS is director of research programs for the Joint Center for Political and Economic Studies. From 1981 to 1986, she was director of the Urban Institute's Minorities and Social Policy Program. Before that, she was a senior research associate in the institute's program of research on women and family policy. Ms. Simms has received several awards, including the Distinguished Achievement Award from the Carleton Alumni Association and the Outstanding Young Woman Award from Fuller and Dees. She received her Ph.D. in economics from Stanford University.

THEDA SKOCPOL is a professor of sociology at Harvard University. Previously, she was a professor of sociology and political science at the University of Chicago. In addition, Professor Skocpol is cochair of the Working Group on States and Social Structures. She currently sits on the editorial board of five journals. Her books include *The Politics of Social Policy in the United States* (co-edited with Margaret Weir and Ann Shola Orloff) and *Protecting Soldiers and Mothers: The Political Origins of Social Policy in the United States*. She is currently working on a book entitled *Social Security Against Welfare*, which deals with U.S. social policies from the 1930s to the present. Professor Skocpol received her Ph.D. in sociology from Harvard University in 1975.

PAUL STARR is a professor of sociology at Princeton University and co-editor of *The American Prospect*. Among his many publications is *The Social Transformation of American Medicine*, which won the Pulitzer Prize, the Bancroft Prize, and the C. Wright Mills award. His latest book is *The Logic of Health Care Reform*. Professor Starr received his Ph.D. from Harvard University.

PAUL N. VAN DE WATER is deputy assistant director for budget analysis at the Congressional Budget Office, with which he has been associated since 1981. From 1979 to 1981, Mr. Van de Water was the acting director of the Office of Policy Analysis at the Social Security

Administration. He has also served as an economist in the Office of the Secretary of Health, Education, and Welfare, a teaching assistant at the Massachusetts Institute of Technology, and a fellow at the Advisory Commission on Intergovernmental Relations. He has written many publications on governmental finance and Social Security and is the editor of *Social Insurance Issues for the Nineties,* published by the National Academy of Social Insurance in 1992. Mr. Van de Water received his Ph.D. in economics from the Massachusetts Institute of Technology in 1975.

BRUCE C. VLADECK has been the president of the United Hospital Fund of New York since 1983. He also sits on the Prospective Payment Assessment Commission, as well as on numerous other commissions and boards at the national, state, and local levels. Mr. Vladeck has previously served as assistant vice president of the Robert Wood Johnson Foundation and assistant commissioner for health planning and resources development for the New Jersey State Department of Health; and he has also taught at Columbia University. He has lectured and written on issues of health care policy, health care financing, and long-term care. Mr. Vladeck is the author of *Unloving Care: The Nursing Home Tragedy,* and of numerous articles and book chapters. He received his Ph.D. from the University of Michigan.

JAMES WEILL is the general counsel of the Children's Defense Fund. Previously, he was deputy director of the Legal Assistance Foundation of Chicago. He has been the attorney in numerous class actions involving AFDC and other means-tested programs, Social Security, and the constitutional rights of welfare recipients, children, and women in the U.S. Court of Appeals and the U.S. Supreme Court. Mr. Weill has written extensively on poverty, income and tax issues, children's rights, and child advocacy. One of his most recent publications is a monograph for UNICEF, *Child Advocacy in the United States: The Work of the Children's Defense Fund.* He received his J.D. from New York University.